QUIZ
YOURSELF
CLEVER!
TREES
OF THE WORLD

Produced for DK by Just Content Limited
10A Little Square, Braintree, Essex, CM7 1UT

Editorial Just Content Limited
Design PDQ Digital Media Solutions, Bungay, UK

Senior editor Shaila Brown
US editor Lori Hand
Senior art editor Jacqui Swan
Managing editor Rachel Fox
Managing art editor Owen Peyton Jones
Production editor Gill Reid
Production controller Joss Moore
Jacket designer Stephanie Tan
Jacket design development manager Sophia MTT
Publisher Andrew Macintyre
Associate publishing director Liz Wheeler
Art director Karen Self
Publishing director Jonathan Metcalf

First American Edition, 2024
Published in the United States by DK Publishing,
a division of Penguin Random House LLC
1745 Broadway, 20th Floor, New York, NY 10019

A catalog record for this book is available
from the Library of Congress.
ISBN: 978-0-5938-4153-2

DK books are available at special discounts when purchased in bulk
for sales promotions, premiums, fund-raising, or educational use.
For details, contact: DK Publishing Special Markets, 1745 Broadway,
20th Floor, New York, NY 10019 or SpecialSales@dk.com

Printed and bound in China

www.dk.com

The name of the Smithsonian Institution and the sunburst logo
are registered trademarks of the Smithsonian Institution.
For more information, please visit www.si.edu

Smithsonian

MIX
Paper | Supporting
responsible forestry
FSC
www.fsc.org   FSC™ C018179

This book was made with Forest
Stewardship Council™ certified
paper — one small step in DK's
commitment to a sustainable future.
Learn more at
www.dk.com/uk/information/sustainability

Contents

How to use this book

Quizzes are one of the best ways to learn new facts and test your knowledge. You can do the quizzes by yourself, with a friend, or in teams.

How to play
Try answering the questions on the right-hand page. You'll find all the answers on the next page. How many questions did you get right? If you want to increase your scores and boost your brain power, reread the profile and test yourself again! If you are playing with friends, you'll need pen and paper to write down the answers. Whoever gets the most correct answers wins!

A description of the tree at the top of the page provides a clue.

The tree's common name and a short introduction are here.

? ? ? **Majestic crown** ? ? ?

What **tree** is this?

How **wide** does it grow?

What **color** are the catkins? ◄ These are the questio about the t

A photo of t tree's featu such as the leaves, fruit and flowers will help you name the species

Is this tree **rare** in Europe?

How **long** does this tree live?

Which **rulers** used to wear crowns of leaves from this tree?

What other **name** is this tree called?

Common oak

Also known as the pedunculate oak, this majestic tree grows best in damp, well-drained soils. The oak has a long lifespan, with many trees more than 1,000 years old. The leaves taper at the base and are usually unstalked. The upper surface is deep green and the underside is blue-green.

The dataset provides some of the answers.

Height 80–130 ft (25–40 m)
Width Up to 100 ft (30 m)
Leaf type Simple
Tree shape Spreading
Location Asia, Africa, Europe

The location is the tree's native country or region.

This oak is a deciduous, spreading tree with smooth shoots. It is the commonest oak across much of Europe.

Roman emperors often wore crowns of oak leaves, associating them with strength and power.

There is a fun fact on each tree profile that may also provide an answer to one of the questions.

The flowers are long, greenish-yellow catkins. The fruit grows on a stalk up to 4 in (10 cm) long.

92

Further details about the tree are given, such as its fruit, leaf shape, flowers, bark, and seeds.

The illustration indicates whether the tree is deciduous (loses its leaves in winter), evergreen, or semi-evergreen.

? ? ? ? **Deciduous**
Quercus robur ? ? ? 91

The tree group and the species' Latin name appear at the bottom of the page to help you guess the tree's identity.

What are trees?

Trees are distinguished from other plants by their upright woody stem, roots, and branches, and by the fact that they do not die back on a regular basis, but continue to grow year after year. They are the largest plants on Earth.

Role of trees
Trees are essential to all life. They absorb vast amounts of carbon dioxide and other pollutants from the atmosphere, replacing them with oxygen. Forests help regulate excess water flow and can reduce the effects of flooding and soil erosion. Trees influence weather patterns by increasing humidity and generating rainfall. They help make our cities and towns green, and provide a habitat for wildlife.

Despite so many obvious values, large swaths of forest are being lost every year, often for commercial gain or farming. More than 8,750 species are threatened with extinction, and across the world, at least 100 acres (40 hectares) of trees are felled every minute of every day.

Rainforest
There are thousands of different rainforest trees. Madagascar alone supports more than 2,000 different species, and there can be up to 500 different species within 2.5 acres (1 hectare) in the Amazon rainforest.

How trees work

The structure of a tree

Each part of a tree has its own unique function. Some parts, such as the trunk and leaves, are clearly visible. Other parts are less obvious, for example, the circulatory system, roots, and, in some species, the reproductive organs.

Seeds
The next generation of trees, seeds contain the basic ingredients for creating new trees virtually identical to their parents. Seeds may be contained in fruits, such as berries.

Leaves
These produce food used by the tree to provide energy for living and growing—by photosynthesis. Leaves are also the site of transpiration (water loss by evaporation).

Flowers
The flowers contain the tree's reproductive organs. Male and female parts may occur within the same flower, or the tree may have separate male and female flowers.

Bark
This is a waterproof layer that surrounds the trunk and branches and protects the interior of the tree. It has tiny pores that allow oxygen to pass into the living cells inside.

Roots
Tree roots provide anchorage and collect the tree's water, minerals, and nutrients from the soil. Roots also store food, in the form of starch, for later use.

Making food

Food, in the form of energy-rich sugars, is supplied through a process called photosynthesis that takes place in leaves. The sugar (sucrose) produced provides energy and can be turned into starch for storage and cellulose for building.

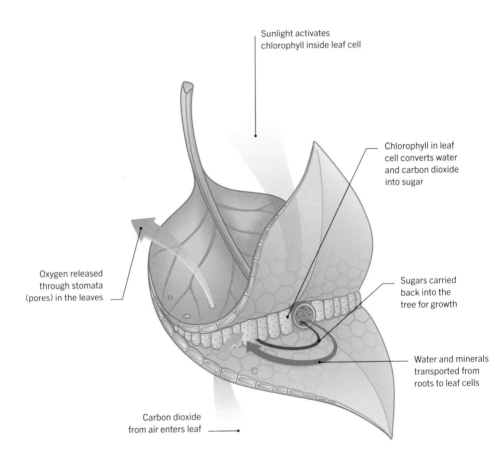

Sunlight activates chlorophyll inside leaf cell

Chlorophyll in leaf cell converts water and carbon dioxide into sugar

Oxygen released through stomata (pores) in the leaves

Sugars carried back into the tree for growth

Water and minerals transported from roots to leaf cells

Carbon dioxide from air enters leaf

Photosynthesis
Chlorophyll, the green pigment in leaves, is activated by light energy from the sun. Tiny pores in the leaf's surface absorb carbon dioxide from the atmosphere. This reacts with water to produce sugar.

Easy-to-spot tree shapes

Tree shapes

The shape of a tree is known as its habit. It can be a good clue to help you identify some trees.

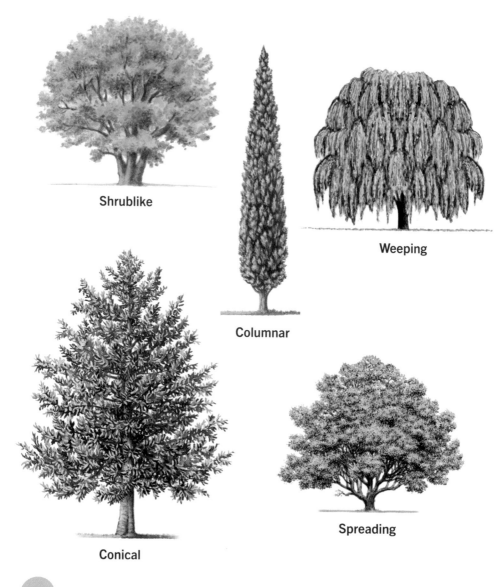

Shrublike

Columnar

Weeping

Conical

Spreading

Easy-to-spot seeds and fruit

Seeds and fruit
The form, shape, size, and color of fruit and seeds are also helpful clues.

Atlas cedar

Plum

Common oak

Take a closer look

Bark
Color, flaking, banding, ridges, and the appearance of lenticels (pores) on the bark can all help you to identify a tree.

Horizontal peeling

Vertical peeling

Irregular plates

Ridged and fissured

Leaf arrangements
Look closely at how the leaves are arranged on the shoot.

Opposite

Alternate

Pinnate

Palmate

Simple leaves
These do not have leaflets and are arranged in one of two ways: opposite, with leaves paired on either side of the stalk, or alternate, with the leaves in a staggered pattern.

Compound leaves
These are divided into leaflets, which may branch from the tip of the stalk (palmate) or may be arranged symmetrically along the stalk's length (pinnate).

Flower types

Determining how a flower is arranged on the stem can help you figure out which tree it is. The most common arrangements are shown here.

Spike

Corymb

Catkin

Raceme

Solitary

Leaf shapes

The most common leaf shapes are shown here, and you will find some of them in this book.

Needle-like   Linear   Scale-like   Oblanceolate

Oblong   Lanceolate   Obovate

Elliptic   Cordate (heart-shaped)   Rounded

Leaf margins

There are lots of different indentations in the leaf margins (edges) that can help you identify a tree. Some are shown here.

Smooth texture
The margins of leaves may be smooth (known as entire), or slightly wavy.

Entire

Wavy

Serrated sides
The edge may be toothed (like the teeth of a saw), or lobed.

Lobed

Toothed

The quiz
starts
here ...

What type of **leaf** does it have?

What **tree** is this?

How **tall** does it grow?

How **long** can the seed cones grow?

Where in the world does this tree grow?

What color is the **bark** when the tree is mature?

Conifers
Abies grandis

15

Grand fir

The grand fir is native to the Pacific Northwest and northern California regions, where specimens regularly reach up to 280 ft (80 m) in height, with a trunk diameter of 6 ft (2 m). Scottish botanist David Douglas came across this tree on an expedition to the United States around 1830.

Height 230–280 ft (70–80 m)

Width Up to 20 ft (6 m)

Leaf type Needle-like

Tree shape Conical

Location North America

The female seed cones are cylindrical and green, up to 4 in (10 cm) long, becoming brown when mature.

The grand fir is an extremely fast-growing tree—it can grow up to 90 cm (35 in) per year.

The brown bark turns purple-gray and cracks into square plates when the tree reaches maturity.

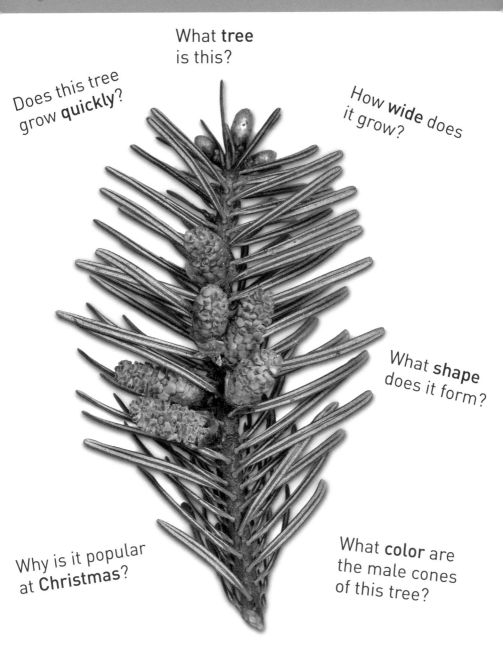

What **tree** is this?

Does this tree grow **quickly**?

How **wide** does it grow?

What **shape** does it form?

Why is it popular at **Christmas**?

What **color** are the male cones of this tree?

Do the leaves **smell** good when they are crushed?

Conifers
Abies nordmanniana

Caucasian fir

This slow-growing conifer has dense branches and a conical outline, which makes it a magnificent specimen in parks and gardens. It is also a popular Christmas tree and, under the name of Nordmann fir, is marketed as a "nondrop" tree, since it retains its needles for some time after being cut.

Height Up to 130 ft (40 m)

Width Up to 15 ft (5 m)

Leaf type Needle-like

Tree shape Conical

Location Asia, Europe

Caucasian firs are native to the Caucasus and northeast Turkey. They are sometimes planted for forestry and grown as Christmas trees.

Male Caucasian fir cones are tinged with red and grow in clusters below the shoot.

The leaves of the Caucasian fir produce a fruity smell when crushed.

What **tree** is this?

What **shape** are the leaves of this tree?

This tree **changes shape** as it grows. True or false?

Where in the **world** does it come from?

Who took this tree to **Europe**?

Where is this tree popular at **Christmas**?

What **color** are the shoots of this tree?

Noble fir

This conifer was taken from North America to Europe by Scottish botanist David Douglas in 1825. Its pale reddish-brown shoots are hidden by flattened leaves that sweep upward at the sides. The leaves have a bluish-green upper surface and two narrow bands of stomata (pores) on their underside.

Height Up to 160 ft (50 m)

Width Up to 20 ft (6 m)

Leaf type Needle-like

Tree shape Columnar

Location North America

The noble fir is the most popular Christmas tree in Denmark.

Narrowly conical when young, the evergreen noble fir becomes columnar with age.

Large green cones are densely covered with long, pointed bracts.

Ancient symbol

What **tree** is this?

How is the **wood** from this tree used?

What **color** is the cone when ripe?

Where in the world does it come from?

How **high** does it grow?

Conifers
Taxus baccata

Common yew

The common yew is an evergreen tree that develops a dense, dark canopy when it reaches maturity. It may grow to be as wide as its height and live to a great age—some trees are believed to be several thousand years old. Yew wood is extremely durable and valued for veneer and furniture production.

Height 50–70 ft (15–20 m)

Width Up to 70 ft (20 m)

Leaf type Needle-like

Tree shape Conical

Location Asia, Europe

The fruit is a single seed, held in a fleshy cone (aril). The aril ripens from green to red.

A common yew called the Fortingall Yew in Scotland is believed to be around 5,000 years old.

The common yew is often seen in gardens as hedges or topiary.

Lifesaver

What **tree** is this?

How **wide** can it become?

What **shape** are the leaves of this tree?

What **color** is its bark?

In what sort of **places** does it grow?

This bark is used for **medicine**. True or false?

Conifers
Taxus brevifolia

23

Pacific yew

This small conifer is native to western North America, from British Columbia to California. It grows in canyons and gullies, often alongside streams. The anticancer drug paclitaxel (Taxol) was isolated from this tree's bark in the 1960s, and it has been used in the treatment of lung and breast cancer ever since.

Height 30–70 ft (10–20 m)

Width Up to 30 ft (10 m)

Leaf type Needle-like

Tree shape Conical

Location North America

The yew's bark is thin, flaky, and reddish-brown in color.

The same chemicals that make the Pacific yew tree a lifesaver can be fatal if eaten.

Juvenile (young) trees tend to be angular, becoming more conical with age. The branches are slender and hang slightly downward.

Arching branches

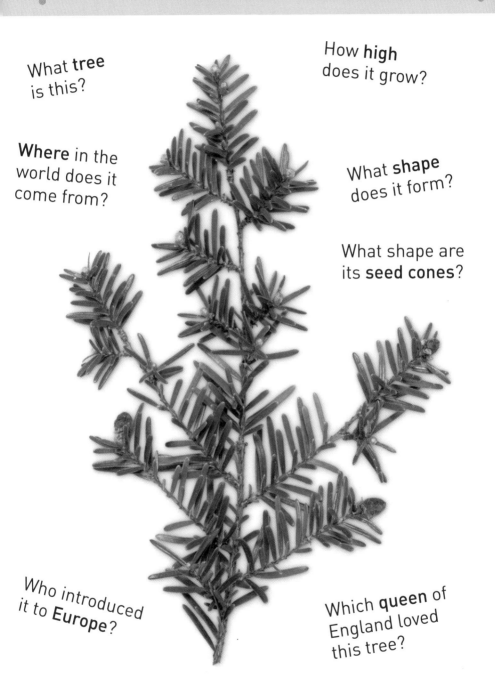

What **tree** is this?

How **high** does it grow?

Where in the world does it come from?

What **shape** does it form?

What shape are its **seed cones**?

Who introduced it to **Europe**?

Which **queen** of England loved this tree?

Western hemlock

Also known as Prince Albert's fir, this tall, elegant conifer is characterized by its spreading, arching branches and soft foliage. The western hemlock is fast-growing and produces strong lumber. Since being introduced to Europe around 1828 by Scottish botanist David Douglas, it has been widely grown on tree farms as a lumber-producing tree.

Height 160–280 ft (50–80 m)

Width Up to 70 ft (20 m)

Leaf type Needle-like

Tree shape Conical

Location North America

The conical western hemlock often has a drooping leading shoot at the top of the tree.

Queen Victoria of England loved this tree and asked for its name to be changed in honor of her husband, Albert.

The mature seed cones are woody, and egg-shaped. They are around 1 in (2.5 cm) long.

What **tree** is this?

Where in the world does it come from?

What color is its **bark**?

How long do female cones take to **mature**?

How are the growing tips **protected** in winter?

This tree was once thought to be **extinct**. True or false?

Is this tree very **common** in the wild?

Conifers
Wollemia nobilis

Wollemi pine

Once thought to have been extinct for at least two million years, a live Wollemi pine was discovered in 1994, growing in a remote canyon in Australia. There are fewer than 100 mature trees in the wild, but thousands have been reproduced from them and are being cultivated around the world.

Height 70–130 ft (20–40 m)

Width Up to 30 ft (10 m)

Leaf type Needle-like

Tree shape Conical

Location Australia

In winter, the growing tips of the buds are protected by a white, waxy coating and the leaves take on a bronze hue.

The Wollemi pine's bark is reddish-brown, and peels in thin scales when young. It develops a chocolate-brown, bubbly texture with age.

Fossils show that Wollemi pine trees grew at the same time as when dinosaurs roamed the Earth.

Female cones are small and green. They take about two years to mature.

Lofty grower

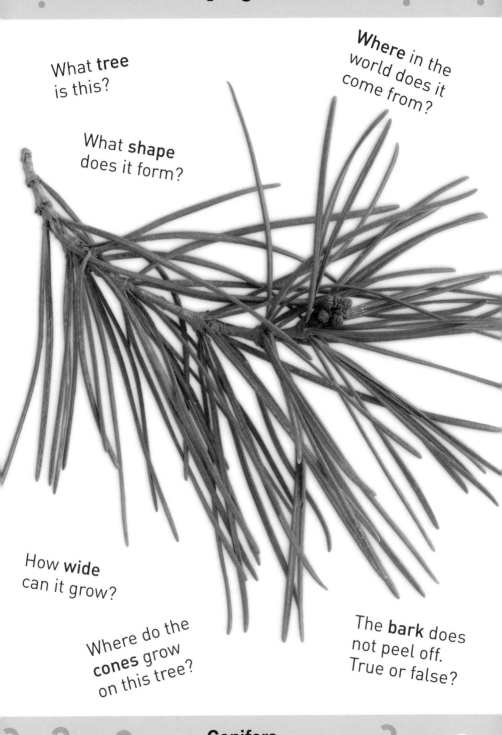

What **tree** is this?

Where in the world does it come from?

What **shape** does it form?

How **wide** can it grow?

Where do the **cones** grow on this tree?

The **bark** does not peel off. True or false?

Japanese umbrella pine

The Japanese umbrella pine grows at elevations of up to 5,000 ft (1,520 m) on rocky slopes and ridges. The leaves grow in umbrella-like whorls, hence the tree's name. Young green cones develop at the ends of each shoot.

Height 70–100 ft (20–30 m)

Width Up to 50 ft (15 m)

Leaf type Needle-like

Tree shape Conical

Location Japan

The bark is dark brown to gray and peels in long, coarse strips.

The egg-shaped mature seed cones are green, turning to woody-brown. They grow up to 3 in (7.5 cm) wide.

The Japanese umbrella pine is very slow growing and is popular as a bonsai tree.

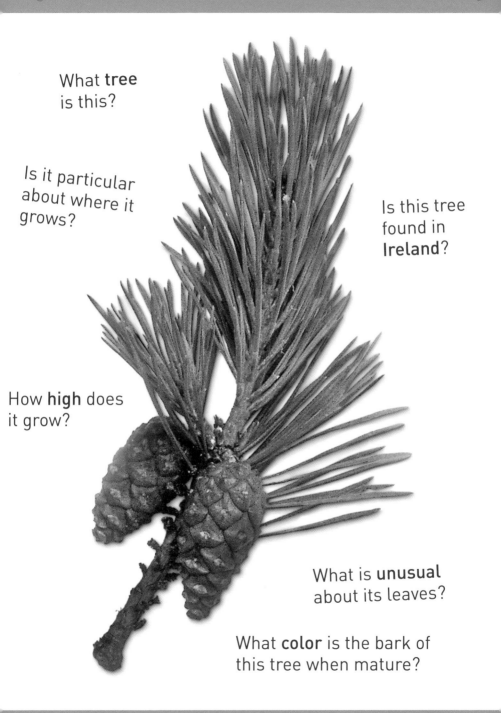

What **tree** is this?

Is it particular about where it grows?

Is this tree found in **Ireland**?

How **high** does it grow?

What is **unusual** about its leaves?

What **color** is the bark of this tree when mature?

Conifers
Pinus sylvestris

Scots pine

The Scots pine's natural range extends from Ireland, across northern Europe and Asia, to the Pacific coast. It can grow on all types of soil, from dry and sandy to wet and peaty. It produces many seeds and is able to colonize new territory quickly. Mature trees develop domed crowns with large, snaking branches.

Height 80–100 ft (25–30 m)

Width Up to 50 ft (15 m)

Leaf type Needle-like

Tree shape Conical

Location Asia, Europe

In Scotland, Scots pine trees form unique forests that are home to rare animals like the red squirrel.

The shoots of the Scots pine bear long, twisted leaves and male and female cones in separate clusters.

The mature bark is flaky with an orange-red tinge.

Cloud reacher

What **tree** is this?

How **wide** can it grow?

This tree is very resistant to **fire**. True or false?

What **color** do the leaves become when they age?

What **shape** does it form?

Does it have **smooth** leaves?

Where in the world does it grow?

Conifers
Pinus canariensis

Canary Island pine

This tree grows naturally in the Canary Islands. It is one of the dominant trees in the Canary Island montane cloud forests, such as those on Mount Teide on Tenerife. Here, its long leaves "comb" low-lying clouds for valuable moisture. Its egg-shaped seed cones are stubby and rough to the touch.

Height 100 ft (30 m)

Width Up to 50 ft (15 m)

Leaf type Needle-like

Tree shape Columnar

Location Canary Islands

This evergreen tree is conical at first, later becoming columnar. It grows on the volcanic mountain slopes of the Canary Islands.

The Canary Island pine is one of the most fire-resistant trees in the world.

Young leaves turn bright grass-green as they age. The margin of each leaf is finely toothed and feels coarse when run through the fingers.

What **tree** is this?

What **shape** are its leaves?

The **branches** always grow close together. True or false?

How did this tree get its **name**?

What causes its **cones** to open?

Does this tree only grow in **warm** places?

How **high** does it grow?

Lodgepole pine

This hardy conifer gets its name from its traditional use by the indigenous peoples of North America for the central pole of their tipis or lodges. The lodgepole pine is able to withstand exposure, cold, and wet soils extremely well. The tree grows straight with defined whorls of branches, sometimes as much as 3 ft (1 m) apart.

Height 20 m (70 ft)

Width Up to 30 ft (10 m)

Leaf type Needle-like

Tree shape Conical

Location North America

Growing in coastal dunes and bogs, the lodgepole pine is broad and bushy near the ground, with branches hanging low at the base of the trunk.

The cones from a lodgepole pine open only when heated by a forest fire, so they can wait years to open.

The leaves grow in pairs and are deep green when young. The brown, oval-shaped cones face down on the branches.

Towering giant

What **tree** is this?

How **high** is the tallest example of this tree?

What **shape** does it have when mature?

Is the bark **hard** or **soft**?

What color **bark** does it have?

It has **speckled** leaves. True or false?

Conifers
Sequoia sempervirens

Coastal redwood

This species bears the distinction of producing the tallest tree in the world—currently 380 ft (115 m) tall. Young coastal redwood trees are conical, with widely spaced, slender branches that curve upward at the tips. The leaves are speckled with two bands of white stomata (pores) on the underside.

Height 130–360 ft (40–110 m)

Width Up to 75 ft (23 m)

Leaf type Needle-like

Tree shape Columnar

Location United States

Mature coastal redwood trees have a columnar shape, with flat tops and downswept branches.

The world's tallest living tree is a coastal redwood in California called Hyperion. It is taller than the Statue of Liberty.

The bark is red-brown, thick, soft, and fibrous.

Drive-through tree

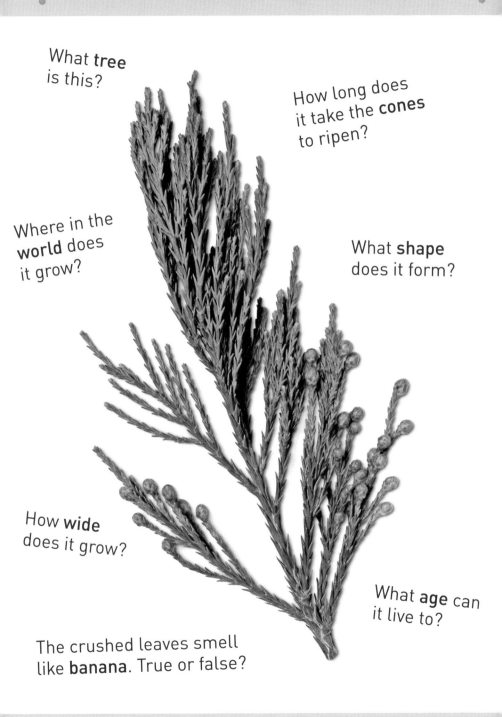

What **tree** is this?

How long does it take the **cones** to ripen?

Where in the **world** does it grow?

What **shape** does it form?

How **wide** does it grow?

What **age** can it live to?

The crushed leaves smell like **banana**. True or false?

Giant redwood

Giant redwoods are long-lived, with some trees believed to be 3,500 years old. They have large, downswept branches and leaves that release a smell of aniseed when crushed. Straight, bright green female cones develop into bunches of drooping, green seed cones. These ripen in two years, becoming brown.

Height 160–310 ft (50–95 m)

Width Up to 50 ft (15 m)

Leaf type Needle-like

Tree shape Columnar

Location United States (California)

Cones are long-stalked, egg-shaped, and up to 2 in (5 cm) wide.

For many years, cars could drive in a tunnel cut through a giant redwood tree in Yosemite National Park.

One of the tallest and widest trees on Earth is a giant redwood called General Sherman, which grows on the western slopes of the Sierra Nevada in California.

Fossil tree

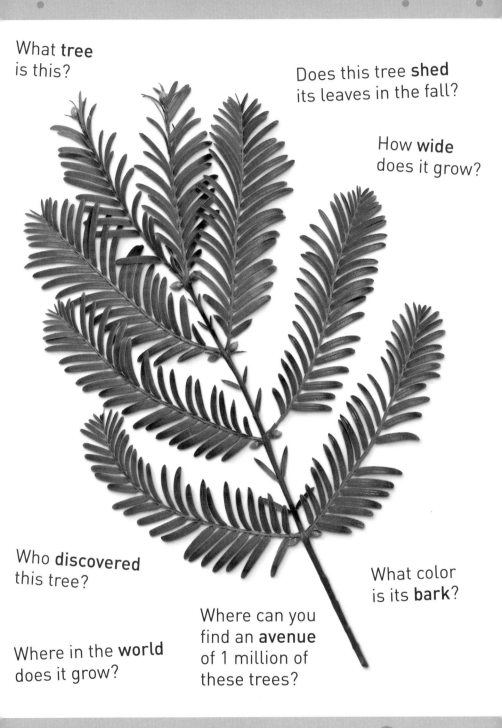

What **tree** is this?

Does this tree **shed** its leaves in the fall?

How **wide** does it grow?

Who **discovered** this tree?

What color is its **bark**?

Where in the **world** does it grow?

Where can you find an **avenue** of 1 million of these trees?

Conifers
Metasequoia glyptostroboides

Dawn redwood

Also referred to as the fossil tree, the dawn redwood tree was discovered in 1941 by Chinese forester T. Kan in eastern Sichuan province. Until then, it had only been seen as a fossil and was believed to have been extinct for many millennia. This conifer has become popular for planting in parks and gardens.

Height Up to 80 ft (25 m)

Width Up to 22 ft (7 m)

Leaf type Needle-like

Tree shape Conical

Location China

The longest dawn redwood avenue in the world is in Pizhou, China, and contains over 1 million trees.

The dawn redwood's bright green leaves turn pink, sometimes gold, in autumn before falling.

The fibrous bark sometimes has a spiraled appearance. It is bright cinnamon-brown and peels in stringy, vertical flakes.

Bald water-lover

What **tree** is this?

How **high** does this tree grow?

This tree has **knees**. True or false?

Why is it **different** than most conifers?

Where in the **world** does it grow?

Are male and female **cones** found on different trees?

Does it prefer **damp** soil?

Swamp cypress

Also known as the bald cypress, this ornamental conifer grows in damp or wet soils. It tolerates having its roots submerged in water for several months at a time by developing aerial roots. The crown of the swamp cypress is conical, becoming slightly domed with age, and has heavy, upswept branches.

Height 100–160 ft (30–50 m)

Width Up to 80 ft (25 m)

Leaf type Needle-like

Tree shape Conical

Location United States

Both male and female cones grow on the same tree. The small, green female seed cones ripen into round, short-stalked, pale brown cones.

Aerial roots known as "knees" rise above water level to absorb oxygen.

This tree is also called the bald cypress because, unlike most conifers, it loses its needles once a year.

What **tree** is this?

What shape are its **leaves**?

The wood from this tree is used to build **boats**. True or false?

Which **herb** do the leaves smell like?

What **color** are the mature seed cones?

What musical **instrument** is this tree used to make?

Lawson cypress

This popular garden conifer is a large, conical tree with drooping branches, and makes an excellent hedge or screen. Originally a forest tree, it remains an important lumber-producing tree. The uses of the Lawson cypress range from boat building to cabinet making.

Height Up to 130 ft (40 m)

Width 30–50 ft (10–15 m)

Leaf type Needle-like

Tree shape Conical

Location United States

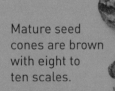

Mature seed cones are brown with eight to ten scales.

The conical, evergreen Lawson cypress has dark green foliage in drooping, flattened sprays. When crushed, the foliage has a distinctive smell of parsley.

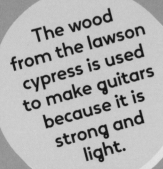

The wood from the lawson cypress is used to make guitars because it is strong and light.

What **tree** is this?

What **shape** does it form?

Where in the **world** does it grow?

Can it grow on **mountains**?

What **color** are the young female cones?

The cones are **smooth** and **slippery** to touch. True or false?

Oriental spruce

Also known as the Caucasian spruce, this graceful tree is one of the best spruces for cultivation, being able to withstand drier conditions. It grows in mountainous regions up to 7,220 ft (2,200 m). Since its cultivation in 1837, it has been widely planted in parks and gardens, especially in the United States.

Height 100–180 ft (30–55 m)

Width Up to 50 ft (15 m)

Leaf type Needle-like

Tree shape Conical

Location Asia, Europe

The blunt leaves are shiny and dark green on the upper surface, paler on the underside, and point forward on pale brown shoots.

In the wild, oriental spruce trees can be as tall as 180 ft (55 m), but are much shorter when grown in a yard.

The cylindrical female cones are purple at first and turn brown as they mature. They are sticky with resin, and fall from the tree when ripe.

Festive tree

What **tree** is this?

How **high** does it grow?

Is it a **symmetrical** shape?

Does it have completely **smooth** bark?

What **time of year** might you see a lot of these trees?

Is it used for making musical **instruments**?

Its leaves have a **citrus** smell. True or false?

Norway spruce

This conifer is recognized as the traditional Christmas tree throughout most of Europe. It is an important lumber-producing tree, used in construction and for making stringed musical instruments. It is symmetrical, with horizontal branches that gradually become upswept toward the top of the tree.

Height Up to 160 ft (50 m)

Width Up to 50 ft (15 m)

Leaf type Needle-like

Tree shape Conical

Location Europe

Male pollen cones cluster at shoot tips, releasing clouds of yellow pollen in spring. When crushed, the rich-green leaves give off a citruslike fragrance.

The slightly rough bark can develop shallow round or oval plates on the surface with age.

Norway provides the cities of London, Edinburgh, and Washington D.C. with a Norway spruce every Christmas.

The Norway spruce is a common spruce in Europe and often used as a Christmas tree.

Mountain dweller

What **tree** is this?

How **wide** does it grow?

Where in the **world** does it grow?

Which part of this tree is used to make **perfume**?

When do the cones shed their **pollen**?

The male and female cones are the same **color**. True or false?

What color is its **bark**?

Atlas cedar

This evergreen conifer is found naturally in the Atlas Mountains of North Africa, where it grows along the snowline around 7,200 ft (2,200 m) above sea level. The Atlas cedar is distinguished by its upswept, ascending branches. Its foliage varies from dark green to light gray-blue in the wild.

Height 100–130 ft (30–40 m)

Width Up to 70 ft (20 m)

Leaf type Needle-like

Tree shape Conical

Location Africa

The oil collected from the needles of the Atlas cedar is used to make perfumes.

Golden male and green female cones grow in separate clusters on the same tree. The male cones, up to 2 in (5 cm) long, shed pollen in autumn before falling to the ground.

The slate-gray bark develops scaly plates when mature.

What **tree** is this?

What **shape** does it form?

Where in the **world** does it grow?

Is it used in **construction**?

Does this tree have **upright** or **drooping** branches?

What is another **name** for this tree?

Conifers
Cedrus deodara

Deodar cedar

The deodar cedar is native to the western Himalayas and is sometimes referred to as the Indian cedar. These huge trees can grow up to 250 ft (75 m) tall and live for close to 1,000 years. Many of these trees have been felled for their durable, light brown timber, which is highly prized for construction.

Height 160–250 ft (50–75 m)

Width Up to 50 ft (15 m)

Leaf type Needle-like

Tree shape Conical

Location Himalayas

This cedar is narrowly conical in shape when young, broadening as it matures. It is distinguished from other cedars by the drooping tips on its branches.

The famous houseboats of Kashmir are made from deodar cedar.

The smooth, dark gray bark develops fissures (slits) with age.

Royal favorite

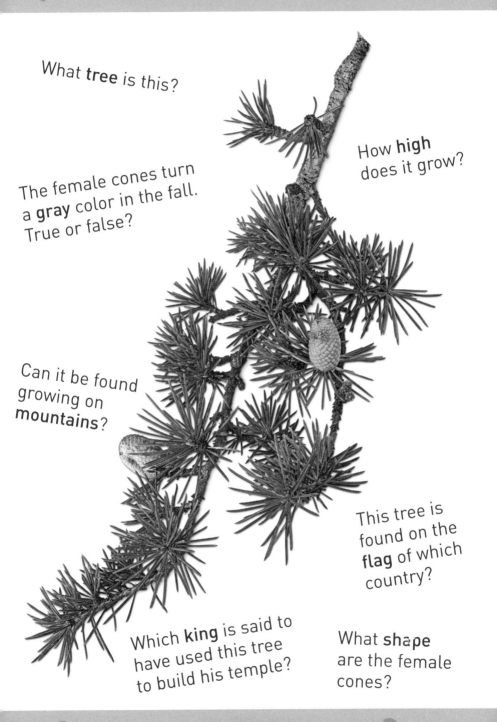

What **tree** is this?

The female cones turn a **gray** color in the fall. True or false?

How **high** does it grow?

Can it be found growing on **mountains**?

This tree is found on the **flag** of which country?

Which **king** is said to have used this tree to build his temple?

What **shape** are the female cones?

Cedar of Lebanon

Among one of the world's best known trees, the cedar of Lebanon has been revered for thousands of years. King Solomon is believed to have built his temple using its timber. On Mount Lebanon, it grows at altitudes of up to 7,020 ft (2,140 m), and is widely planted as an ornamental species.

Height 100–130 ft (30–40 m)

Width Up to 70 ft (20 m)

Leaf type Needle-like

Tree shape Columnar

Location Middle East

This evergreen tree is conical when young, but with age develops its characteristic broad head with flattened and layered branches.

The Cedar of Lebanon features on the Lebanese flag, one of the few flags to feature a tree.

The egg-shaped female cones are pale green, developing a rose-purple tint by early falls.

Prickly needles

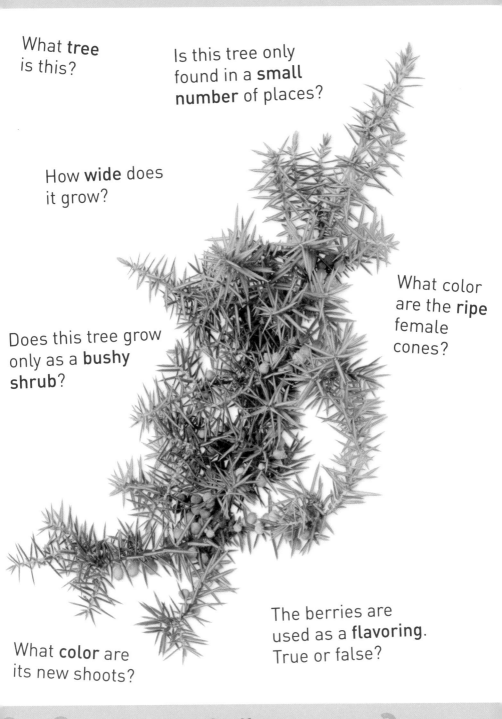

What **tree** is this?

Is this tree only found in a **small number** of places?

How **wide** does it grow?

What color are the **ripe** female cones?

Does this tree grow only as a **bushy shrub**?

The berries are used as a **flavoring**. True or false?

What **color** are its new shoots?

Common juniper

The common juniper is believed to be the most widespread tree in the world. Its natural range extends from Alaska, Greenland, Iceland, and Siberia southward through most of Europe, temperate Asia, and North America. New shoots are blue-green, and may become dark red-brown with age.

Height Up to 15 ft (5 m)

Width Up to 12 ft (4 m)

Leaf type Needle-like

Tree shape Varies

Location Asia, Europe, North America

This evergreen conifer can be a tree, a bushy shrub, or flat and creeping. Many varieties are grown in gardens.

Juniper berries are used to flavor food and drink.

Female seed cones, called juniper berries, ripen to blue-black over two to three years.

What **tree** is this?

Which **continent** does this tree grow in?

Can it survive at **high altitudes**?

Does it have **bending** shoot tips?

How **high** does it grow?

What **color** bark does it have?

Are male and female **cones** found on different trees?

Conifers
Juniperus squamata

Himalayan juniper

Also known as the flaky juniper or the scaly-leaved Nepal juniper, this tree ranges from a low-lying shrub to a small, bushy tree. All forms have bending shoot tips, which is a distinct feature of this species. The red-brown, papery bark flakes in large scales. Male and female cones usually grow on separate trees.

Height 1–90 ft (0.15–28 m)

Width Up to 8 ft (2.5 m)

Leaf type Needle-like

Tree shape Varies

Location Asia

This tree is named after the Himalayas in Asia, where it grows on some of the highest mountains in the world.

Female cones develop into round to egg-shaped berrylike structures, up to ⅜ in (9 mm) long. Initially reddish-brown, they become glossy purple-black when mature. Each cone contains a single seed.

Gilded pretender

What **tree** is this?

How **wide** does it grow?

Does this tree grow **quickly** or **slowly**?

Do its cones **fall** off the tree?

What **shape** does it form?

Where in the **world** does it grow?

What color **bark** does it have?

Golden larch

Despite the name, the beautiful, slow-growing golden larch is not a true larch—its cones disintegrate on the tree and its spurs (side shoots) lengthen every year. It has gray-brown bark and pale yellow to pink-brown shoots. The leaves grow in clusters and turn orange-gold in autumn before falling. Both male and female cones develop on the same tree.

Height 120–150 ft (35–45 m)

Width Up to 50 ft (15 m)

Leaf type Needle-like

Tree shape Conical

Location China

This tree's scientific name, *pseudolarix*, means "fake larch."

The golden larch has a conical habit, with level branches that curve upward toward the tips.

Female seed cones mature only after long, hot summers. Each cone is green, maturing to golden brown before disintegrating on the tree.

What **tree** is this?

Is this a **deciduous** or **evergreen** tree?

What shape **leaf** does it have?

Do its **leaves** change color in the fall?

Where in the **world** does it grow?

What **color** are the female flowers?

Japanese larch

This deciduous tree is characterized by slender and soft, blue- to gray-green leaves that open in early spring, turning yellow in the fall. Male flower clusters are yellow, on the undersides of the shoots, while upright, creamy to pink female flowers are arranged in larger clusters on top of the shoots.

Height Up to 120 ft (35 m)

Width Up to 50 ft (15 m)

Leaf type Needle-like

Tree shape Conical

Location Japan

This tree grows at altitudes of up to 9,020 ft (2,750 m) in the wild. It is also grown in and around Japanese temple gardens, where it may be trained as a bonsai.

Because Japanese larch wood is tough, it is often used in construction and to build furniture.

The leaves are bright green at first, dulling to gray-green before turning yellow in the fall.

Spiky leaves

What **tree** is this?

What shape **leaf** does it have?

Are male and female **flowers** found on different trees?

Which **country** has this tree as its national tree?

What color **bark** does it have?

How **high** does it grow?

Conifers
Araucaria araucana

Monkey puzzle tree

Also known as the Chile pine, the distinctive monkey puzzle tree has shoots that are densely covered by oval, glossy, dark-green leaves ending in sharp points. Male and female flowers are arranged on separate trees—the cylindrical males on side shoots, the rounded females at the ends of the shoots.

Height Up to 100 ft (30 m)

Width Up to 50 ft (15 m)

Leaf type Triangular

Tree shape Spreading

Location Chile, Argentina

Mature trees have cylindrical, tapering trunks, with a light gray bark that is slightly wrinkled. The trunk has whorls of horizontal branches emerging at regular intervals. Overlapping leaves often remain attached to the trunk for many years.

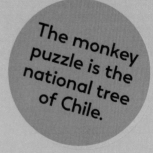

The monkey puzzle is the national tree of Chile.

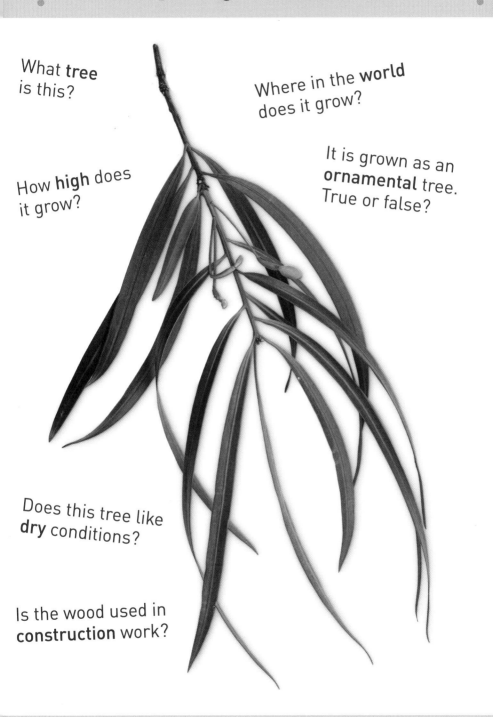

What **tree** is this?

Where in the **world** does it grow?

It is grown as an **ornamental** tree. True or false?

How **high** does it grow?

Does this tree like **dry** conditions?

Is the wood used in **construction** work?

Conifers
Podocarpus salignus

Willow-leaf podocarp

The willow-leaf podocarp is popular as an ornamental tree. However, the wild population in Chile is now vulnerable due to habitat loss and logging for its strong timber, which is used in construction work. This tree thrives on large amounts of rainfall.

Height 50–70 ft (15–20 m)

Width Up to 30 ft (10 m)

Leaf type Needle-like

Tree shape Varies

Location Chile

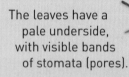

The leaves have a pale underside, with visible bands of stomata (pores).

Willow-leaf podocarp stems can stay fresh for a long time once cut, making it popular in flower bouquets.

The tree's leaf shape and frame, similar to the willow, give the willow-leaf podocarp its name.

What **tree** is this?

What **color** do the leaves turn in autumn?

Does it still grow in the **wild**?

The ripe fruit has a smell similar to **animal poop**. True or false?

This tree has existed since the **Cretaceous** period. True or false?

When was it **introduced** in the West?

Is it used in **medicines**?

Maidenhair tree

Fossil records indicate that this tree has existed on Earth since the Jurassic period, about 200 million years ago. It is no longer found in the wild, but the presence of ancient cultivated trees in southeast China suggests that the last wild population grew in this area. It was introduced in the West in 1730.

Height Up to 130 ft (40 m)

Width Up to 70 ft (20 m)

Leaf type Fan-shaped

Tree shape Conical

Location China

When this tree's fruit starts to rot, it smells like animal poop!

Fleshy, yellow-green seed husks are up to 1½ in (4 cm) long.

The leaves, which have medicinal properties, turn yellow in the fall.

The maidenhair is planted as an ornamental tree throughout the northern hemisphere.

Nighttime flowers

This flower grows on which **tree**?

What fruit do its flowers **smell** like?

Why do **elephants** rip the bark?

How does the tree **store** water?

Which **animal** is its main pollinator?

In which country has this tree been used as a **post office**?

Deciduous
Adansonia digitata

African baobab

Several of the African baobab's largest specimens are believed to be more than 1,000 years old. The tree may remain bare for more than half the year. Its flowers open at night to release a strong scent like that of an overripe melon, which is attractive to fruit bats—the tree's primary pollinator.

Height 30–80 ft (10–25 m)

Width Up to 100 ft (30 m)

Leaf type Simple

Tree shape Spreading

Location Africa, Arabian Peninsula

The African baobab tree stores water in its trunk, ready for the dry season when there is very little rainfall. Elephants sometimes rip the bark to get at the damp wood.

A baobab in Namibia has been used as a post office and a chapel, and can fit at least 35 people inside.

The fruit hangs on long stalks. It contains up to 30 seeds, surrounded by an acidic, edible pulp.

What **tree** is this?

Does it grow better in **cold** regions?

What **color** is its bark?

How **high** does it grow?

It is used to make **traditional medicines**. True or false?

How long does its **fruit** take to ripen?

Common fig

One of the earliest cultivated trees, the small and shrubby but broadly-spreading common fig originates in southwest Asia. However, it is grown throughout warm regions of the world for its edible fruit. The fruit has also been used in Greco-Roman, Islamic, Ayurvedic, and traditional Chinese medicine.

Height Up to 30 ft (10 m)

Width Up to 30 ft (10 m)

Leaf type Simple

Tree shape Spreading

Location Asia

The bark is mid-gray and smooth, with some patterning in old age. The trunk is short and sometimes twisted, while the branches are long, starting from low down on the trunk.

There are about 900 species of fig tree, and each has an individual species of fig wasp to pollinate it.

The fruit is produced in summer near the tips of the shoots. Green in the first year, the fruit ripens over two years.

Sticky leaves

What **tree** is this?

Where in the **world** does it grow?

Does this tree grow **quickly** or **slowly**?

What is another **name** for this tree?

What shape is its **fruit**?

It has **star-shaped** leaves. True or false?

Deciduous
Paulownia tomentosa

Foxglove tree

Also known as the princess tree, this fast-growing, medium-sized, deciduous tree has become popular for planting in parks and yards. The soft leaves are up to 18 in (45 cm) long and wide. They are dark green on the upper surface, lighter on the underside, and covered in fine, sticky hairs.

Height Up to 70 ft (20 m)

Width Up to 40 ft (12 m)

Leaf type Simple

Tree shape Columnar

Location China

The fruit is light green, pointed, and egg-shaped. When ripe, it turns brown.

The leaves are large and heart-shaped at the base, with a shallow lobe on either side.

The soft, light seeds of this tree were used to protect fragile items before polystyrene was invented.

The foxglove tree is rounded to broadly columnar with very stout shoots that are hairy when young.

Stunning color

What **tree** is this?

How **high** does it grow?

Is it a popular **garden** plant?

Is the **bark** rough or smooth?

This tree can get **sunburnt**. True or false?

What time of year does it **flower**?

Deciduous
Acer palmatum

Japanese maple

The Japanese maple tree was first known to Europeans in 1783. However, a trade ban with Japan delayed its introduction into western cultivation until 1820. Today, the maple tree is planted throughout the world and has given rise to hundreds of different garden varieties. It has a smooth bark, even in maturity.

Height 25–50 ft (8–15 m)

Width Up to 30 ft (10 m)

Leaf type Simple

Tree shape Spreading

Location Asia

Japanese maples can get sunburnt if watered on a very hot, sunny day.

In spring, as new leaves emerge, small burgundy-red flowers with yellow stamens appear in upright clusters, becoming droopy later.

The leaves turn bright red, orange, or yellow in the fall. The autumn color is further enhanced by the green or red-winged fruit.

What **tree** is this?

This tree provides food for which **animals**?

Which **country** has its leaf on the flag?

Does it prefer **damp** or **dry** soils?

This tree provides which **sweet** food?

What **color** does it turn in the fall?

Red maple

The large, broadly columnar red maple is normally found growing in deep, damp soils. It has a natural range from eastern Newfoundland and Ontario in Canada to Florida and Texas in the United States. The leaves have three or five lobes with dull blue-green, almost white, undersides, and yellow hairs around the leaf veins.

Height Up to 100 ft (30 m)

Width Up to 50 ft (15 m)

Leaf type Simple

Tree shape Columnar

Location Canada, United States

Canada's most popular emblem is the red maple leaf, which is featured on the country's flag. Quebec, in Canada, is the world's largest producer of maple syrup, which is made from the sap of maple trees.

Moose, deer, and rabbits all eat parts of the red maple tree.

The striking red maple is one of the main elements of the fall leaf color displays.

Helicopter seeds

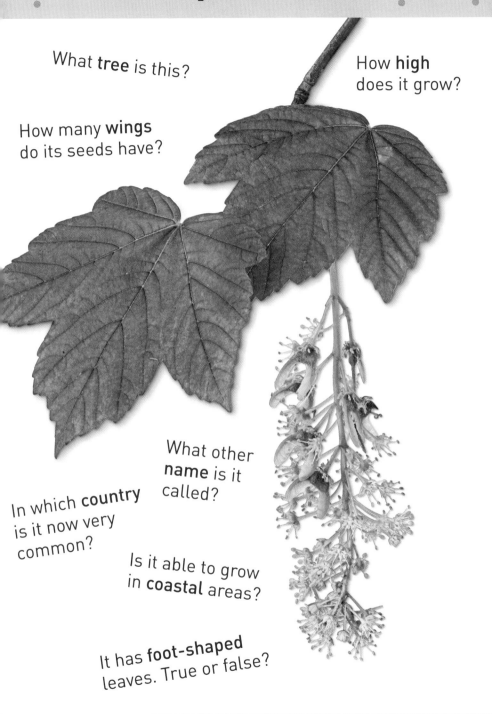

What **tree** is this?

How **high** does it grow?

How many **wings** do its seeds have?

What other **name** is it called?

In which **country** is it now very common?

Is it able to grow in **coastal** areas?

It has **foot-shaped** leaves. True or false?

Deciduous
Acer pseudoplatanus

Sycamore

In some parts of the world this large, broadly columnar tree is known as the plane tree. Although not native to the UK, it is now extremely common there, having become naturalized many centuries ago. A hardy tree, the sycamore is resistant to strong winds and exposure to salty air in coastal regions.

Height 100 ft (30 m)

Width Up to 70 ft (20 m)

Leaf type Simple

Tree shape Columnar

Location Europe

Its gray bark is smooth at first, becoming grayish-pink in maturity with irregular flaking plates.

In autumn, the winged seeds fall from the tree and spiral through the air like helicopters.

The hand-shaped (palmate) leaves have five lobes. They have a deep green upper surface and pale green underside. Two-winged seeds appear in early summer.

What **tree** is this?

How **wide** does it grow?

Does it have **flaky** bark?

What color are the **anthers** that appear in winter?

The leaves turn brown in **fall**. True or false?

Its wood is so strong that it's compared to which **metal**?

Deciduous
Parrotia persica

Persian ironwood

This tree is popular in cultivation because of its beautiful fall leaf color. In the wild Persian ironwood grows upright, reaching 70 ft (20 m) tall. In cultivation, it is broadly spreading, reaching 50 ft (15 m) in height. The branches form a tangled network down to the ground, making it difficult to walk beneath the canopy.

Height 30–70 ft (10–20 m)

Width Up to 50 ft (15 m)

Leaf type Simple

Tree shape Spreading

Location Asia

The bark is dark brown and smooth. It flakes in patches to reveal light fawn-colored new bark.

The leaves transform into beautiful shades of yellow, orange, red, and purple in the fall.

This tree gets gets its name from its dense and strong wood, which can be used to build bridges.

Small clusters of ruby-red anthers, which contain pollen, appear on the bare branches in winter.

Fluffy seeds

What **tree** is this?

Is this tree **endangered** in some parts of the world?

Does its bark have a **heart-shaped** pattern?

Does it grow well in **damp** places?

The **male** and **female** flowers grow on separate trees. True or false?

What color is its **fruit**?

Deciduous
Populus nigra

Black poplar

The large, deciduous, broadly spreading black poplar tree inhabits river valleys and damp areas throughout most of its natural range. It has long, heavy branches and its leaves grow from large, conical, shiny buds. In late spring, tiny seeds, covered in white, cottonlike hairs, are released from green fruit.

Height Up to 100 ft (30 m)

Width Up to 80 ft (25 m)

Leaf type Simple

Tree shape Spreading

Location Asia, Europe

The bark is pale gray, dark, and has a diamond-shaped pattern. It develops large burrs (rough edges) with age.

Male and female flowers grow on separate trees. Male flowers are gray with red anthers, developing drooping catkins in early spring.

Black poplar trees are endangered in Britain—there are about 600 female trees left in the wild.

Trembling leaves

What **tree** is this?

Hundreds of young trees can spring up from the **roots** of the same parent tree. True or false?

What **color** are its catkins?

Which **animal** uses this tree to make its home?

How **high** does it grow?

Does this tree have **red** bark?

Deciduous
Populus tremula

Aspen

Also known as the European aspen, this medium-sized deciduous tree has leaves that tremble in the slightest breeze, hence its species name *tremula*. Aspen is conical when young, becoming broadly spreading with age. It has light and dark gray smooth bark, which becomes ridged at the base in maturity.

Height Up to 70 ft (20 m)

Width Up to 50 ft (15 m)

Leaf type Simple

Tree shape Spreading

Location Asia, Africa, Europe

Drooping gray catkins appear on trees before the leaves emerge in late winter or early spring.

Beavers use the light, strong aspen tree for building their lodges.

Once a tree is established, it grows many offshoots from its roots. Each offshoot is capable of growing into a new tree, so entire groves can be made up of clones of a single tree.

What **tree** is this?

Does it have **flaky** bark?

What **shape** does it form?

Does this tree grow in the **wild**?

It has smooth **fruit**. True or false?

Why is this tree able to live well in **cities**?

Deciduous
Platanus x acerifolia

London plane

The London plane is considered to be an artificially created hybrid between the oriental plane and the American buttonwood. It can withstand both atmospheric pollution and pruning, and is therefore found in many cities. The leaves have a bright green upper surface but are paler on the underside.

Height 100–130 ft (30–40 m)

Width Up to 100 ft (30 m)

Leaf type Simple

Tree shape Columnar

Location Europe

The fruits are bristly spheres that remain attached to the tree well after the leaves have fallen.

Its bark is light brown, often with other colors, flaking in irregular scales.

The London plane is never found growing in the wild.

The London plane is a large, broadly columnar, hybrid tree of garden origin.

Majestic crown

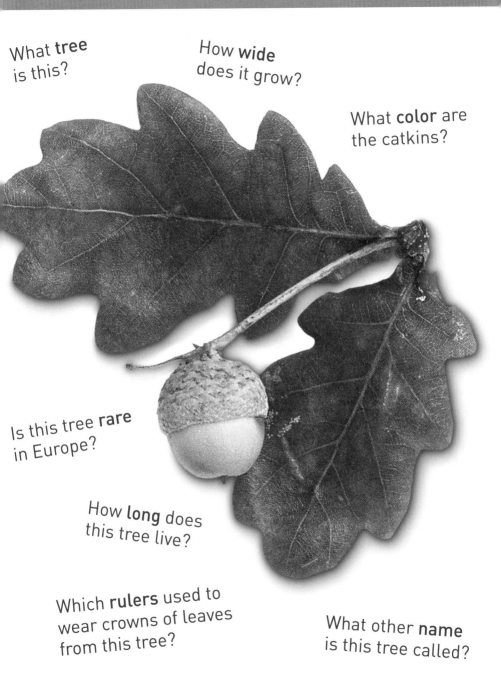

What **tree** is this?

How **wide** does it grow?

What **color** are the catkins?

Is this tree **rare** in Europe?

How **long** does this tree live?

Which **rulers** used to wear crowns of leaves from this tree?

What other **name** is this tree called?

Deciduous
Quercus robur

Common oak

Also known as the pedunculate oak, this majestic tree grows best in damp, well-drained soils. The oak has a long lifespan, with many trees more than 1,000 years old. The leaves taper at the base and are usually unstalked. The upper surface is deep green and the underside is blue-green.

Height 80–130 ft (25–40 m)

Width Up to 100 ft (30 m)

Leaf type Simple

Tree shape Spreading

Location Asia, Africa, Europe

This oak is a deciduous, spreading tree with smooth shoots. It is the commonest oak across much of Europe.

Roman emperors often wore crowns of oak leaves, associating them with strength and power.

The flowers are long, greenish-yellow catkins. The fruit grows on a stalk up to 4 in (10 cm) long.

What **tree** is this?

Does this tree grow **quickly** or **slowly**?

What **color** are its flowers?

What are its **fruits** called?

What part of the tree is eaten by **birds**?

Its flowers are used to make garlands at **Christmas**. True or false?

Does this tree grow in **cold, windy** places?

Common hawthorn

This slow-growing tree is often found in hedges and on open land, although it will grow on the edge of woods, too. Extremely hardy, it can withstand strong winds and cold temperatures. A hawthorn hedge makes an effective windbreak, with its strong mesh of small, thorny branches.

Height Up to 40 ft (12 m)

Width 20 ft (6 m)

Leaf type Simple

Tree shape Shrublike

Location Europe

Common hawthorn flowers were used to make garlands for May Day in the United Kingdom.

The hawthorn's creamy white flowers are followed by small, berrylike fruit, known as haws. Initially green, haws ripen to red in the fall. They remain on the tree well into winter, when they become a valuable food source for migrating birds.

What **tree** is this?

Which **city** is built on lumber from this tree?

Does this tree grow in **Europe**?

Which **animal** likes to nest in the roots of this tree?

This tree always has smooth **bark**. True or false?

Can this tree create its own **oxygen** supply?

Deciduous
Alnus glutinosa

Common alder

This broadly conical tree is normally found growing in damp soil, often close to rivers and lakes. When its roots are submerged in water for long periods of time, it is able to create its own oxygen supply. Its water-durable lumber has been used to make the timber piles upon which Venice, Italy, is built.

Height Up to 80 ft (25 m)

Width Up to 40 ft (12 m)

Leaf type Simple

Tree shape Conical

Location Asia, Africa, Europe

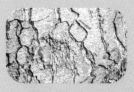

The tree has gray-brown bark, which is lightly cracked from an early age.

The brown cones have scales that open to release numerous seeds.

The common alder's leaves are a shiny dark green on the upper surface and pale gray-green on the underside.

The roots of this tree make it the perfect nesting site for otters.

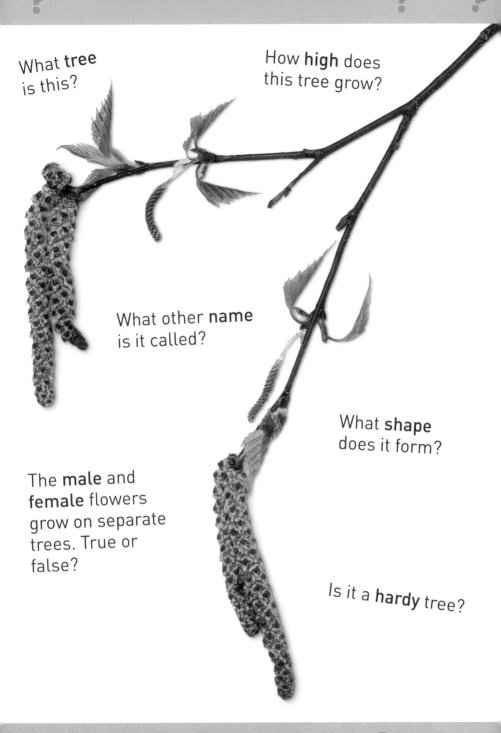

What **tree** is this?

How **high** does this tree grow?

What other **name** is it called?

What **shape** does it form?

The **male** and **female** flowers grow on separate trees. True or false?

Is it a **hardy** tree?

Deciduous
Betula pendula

Silver birch

The narrowly weeping silver birch tree is conical with upswept branches when young. It is hardy, being able to withstand intense cold and long periods of drought. It seeds extensively to establish itself. Also known as the warty birch, it has shoots covered in wartlike bumps, which are rough to the touch.

Height Up to 100 ft (30 m)

Width Up to 20 ft (6 m)

Leaf type Simple

Tree shape Conical

Location Asia, Europe

Both male and female flowers appear separately on the same tree in spring. The male flowers grow in dangling clusters.

A species of woodpecker called the sapsucker pecks into birch tree bark and drinks the sap.

White or silver-gray, the silver birch's bark becomes like cork with black fissures (cracks) in old age.

Bristly fruit

What **tree** is this?

In which **century** was it introduced in western Europe?

Are the leaves **smooth** or **serrated**?

Are the leaves **darker** on the upper or lower surface?

Why is it often planted along the side of **streets**?

Does it have **edible** fruit?

Deciduous
Corylus colurna

Turkish hazel

This tree is native to southeastern Europe and western Asia. It was introduced into cultivation in western Europe in the 16th century, and has been widely planted in parks and gardens since then. With its symmetrical, broadly conical form, the Turkish hazel is ideally suited as an avenue or street tree.

Height Up to 80 ft (25 m)

Width 50 ft (15 m)

Leaf type Simple

Tree shape Conical

Location Asia, Europe

In cultivation, the Turkish hazel normally has a short, straight trunk with a pyramid-shaped canopy.

The Turkish hazel fruit, covered in long bristles, is edible and delicious.

The leaves have a dark green upper surface and are paler on the underside. Each leaf is irregularly serrated.

Angular branches

What **tree** is this?

What did the **Romans** make from the wood of this tree?

Where in the **world** does it grow?

Which other tree does it look **similar** to?

What color do its leaves turn in **the fall**?

How **high** does it grow?

Does it change **shape** as it gets older?

Deciduous
Carpinus betulus

Common hornbeam

This tree is sometimes confused with the common beech. But the trunk and branches of the hornbeam are distinctively angular, unlike those of the beech. The hornbeam's serrated leaves have a dark green upper surface and pale green underside. In the fall, they turn yellow.

Height Up to 100 ft (30 m)

Width Up to 70 ft (20 m)

Leaf type Simple

Tree shape Spreading

Location Asia, Europe

The small, brown nuts at the center of the three-lobed fruit bracts ripen to yellowish-beige in the fall.

Common hornbeam wood is extremely strong and may have been used by the Romans to make their chariots.

Conical when young, the common hornbeam develops a more rounded outline, the slender shoots often drooping at the tips.

Ghostly flowers

What **tree** is this?

It is also known as the **snow** tree. True or false?

How **wide** does it grow?

When does it **flower**?

What happens to its leaves in **hot** weather?

What color is its **fruit**?

Deciduous
Davidia involucrata

Handkerchief tree

This tree is also known as the dove tree or ghost tree. All three names refer to the hanging white bracts, which surround the flowers in spring. The brown bark, initially smooth, develops orange-brown fissures. Shiny, bright green leaves curl in hot or dry weather to reduce water loss.

Height Up to 80 ft (25 m)

Width Up to 50 ft (15 m)

Leaf type Simple

Tree shape Varies

Location China

In spring, the flower bracts are plentiful on this large, broadly conical, sometimes spreading tree.

The name dove tree refers to how the flowers look like doves resting on the branches.

The fruit (a single, green, circular husk) hangs on a stalk about 1½ in (4 cm) long. It contains a hard nut with several seeds inside.

What **tree** is this?

Which **disease** affects this tree?

The wood from this tree is used to make **water pipes**. True or false?

Does it have **smooth** bark?

Which **artist** widely featured this tree in paintings?

How many pairs of **veins** do its leaves have?

Deciduous
Ulmus procera

105

English elm

Native to southwestern Europe, this large, broadly columnar tree was once an important part of the scenery in England, and featured widely in the paintings of English landscape artists such as John Constable. Dutch elm disease led to the destruction of most English elm trees from the 1960s to 1980s.

Height 100–120 ft (30–35 m)

Width Up to 70 ft (20 m)

Leaf type Simple

Tree shape Columnar

Location Europe

The leaves are dark green on the upper surface and pale green on the underside, each with 10–12 pairs of veins.

Tough and water resistant, elm wood was used in England to make water pipes.

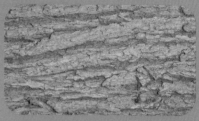

The English elm has a gray-brown bark, which becomes regularly cracked into rough rectangular plates from an early age.

What **tree** is this?

What other **name** is it called?

Is the fruit **edible**?

The **male** and **female** flowers grow on separate trees. True or false?

Has the fruit of this tree been used in traditional **medicine**?

Where in the **world** does it grow?

Deciduous
Celtis occidentalis

Hackberry

Also known as the nettle tree, the leaves of the hackberry look very similar to the leaves of the common stinging nettle (*Urtica dioica*). This medium-sized, columnar, deciduous tree is native to most of North America. It has been widely cultivated in Europe and elsewhere since the 17th century.

Height Up to 80 ft (25 m)

Width Up to 70 ft (20 m)

Leaf type Simple

Tree shape Columnar

Location North America

Male and female flowers appear separately on the same tree in spring. They are followed by fruit that hangs singly on thin, green stalks up to 1 in (2.5 cm) long.

The Iroquois of northeastern North America used hackberries as a source of medicine.

The bark is light gray and smooth when young, developing wartlike blemishes in maturity.

Hedge hero

What **tree** is this?

How **high** does it grow?

Why is it used for **hedges**?

Early **manuscripts** were written on wood from this tree. True or false?

What **color** are its flowers?

Which **animals** eat its seeds?

Deciduous
Fagus sylvatica

Common beech

This majestic, broadly spreading tree is also known as the European beech. In northern Europe, early manuscripts were written on thin tablets of beech wood and bound in beech boards. Nowadays, it is widely used for hedges because it keeps its dead brown leaves throughout winter and provides shelter.

Height Up to 130 ft (40 m)

Width Up to 70 ft (20 m)

Leaf type Simple

Tree shape Spreading

Location Europe, Russia

Yellow-green flowers appear in spring. Both male and female flowers grow on the same tree.

New leaves are yellow-green, covered in fine hairs. Older leaves are tougher.

The seeds of the common beech are eaten by mice, voles, squirrels, and birds.

Sweet-smelling leaves

What **tree** is this?

Does it grow **quickly** or **slowly**?

Does it grow in **Antarctica**?

What do its crushed leaves **smell** like?

The leaves turn brown in **the fall**. True or false?

Does it have **matte** or **glossy** leaves?

Deciduous
Nothofagus antarctica

Antarctic beech

The fast-growing Antarctic beech is broadly columnar. Its bark is dark gray-brown, cracking into irregular plates from an early age. The crown can be quite open, with branches that may be large and sometimes twisted. The shoots are olive-gray on the underside, with a slight covering of hairs.

Height Up to 50 ft (15 m)

Width Up to 30 ft (10 m)

Leaf type Simple

Tree shape Columnar

Location South America

The Mapuche of Chile and Argentina call this tree ñire, which means "fox", because foxes often burrow under it.

Antarctic beech leaves have a deep glossy green upper surface and a paler underside, with four pairs of parallel veins. When crushed, they may release a honeylike fragrance. In the fall, they turn orange, red, and yellow before falling.

Long-living tree

What **tree** is this?

How **high** does this tree grow?

How is this tree important in the production of **silk**?

What **color** is its bark?

Does the fruit from this tree taste **sweet** or **sour**?

Some trees are over **500 years old**. True or false?

Black mulberry tree

Originally from western Asia, the black mulberry reached the British Isles in the early 16th century, and North America after. This tree has been popular for its edible fruit. Several trees are known to be more than 500 years old. Its orange-brown bark becomes cracked from an early age.

Height 25–30 ft (8–10 m)

Width 25–30 ft (8–10 m)

Leaf type Simple

Tree shape Spreading

Location Asia

A broadly spreading tree, the black mulberry has an old appearance from a relatively early age.

Male and female flowers normally grow on separate trees. These are followed by raspberrylike, sweet-tasting fruit on female trees.

For over 5,000 years, humans have grown this tree to rear silkworms that feed on its leaves.

Sour fruit

What **tree** is this?

Is this a **small** or **large** tree?

Which English **writer** mentioned these fruit in his plays?

Can you eat the **raw** fruit?

What **color** are its flowers?

How **wide** can it grow?

Deciduous
Malus sylvestris

Common crab apple tree

This small, spreading tree is also known as the sour apple tree because of the acidic taste of its small fruit, which are inedible when tasted raw. This fruit can, however, be made into a crab apple jelly. This tree has an uneven, low-domed crown of dense, twisting branches, normally leaning to one side.

Height Up to 30 ft (10 m)

Width Up to 20 ft (6 m)

Leaf type Simple

Tree shape Spreading

Location Asia, Europe

The flowers develop into a fruit with creamy white flesh inside, which surrounds a central core containing dark, oval seeds.

The flowers of the common crab apple emerge white, or white flushed with pink, in spring. They are carried in loose clusters on side shoots.

English playwright William Shakespeare wrote about drinks made from crab apples in his plays.

What **tree** is this?

How many **petals** does its flower have?

How **high** does it grow?

Which **American state** is famous for orchards of this tree?

The bark of this tree peels off in **flakes**. True or false?

How many different **types** of this tree have been cultivated?

Cultivated apple tree

Also known as the orchard apple tree, this is a small, broadly spreading tree grown throughout the world for its edible fruit. The apple tree was originally cultivated in western Asia and today there are more than 7,500 known cultivars, each one producing a slightly different fruit, flower, form, or size.

Height Up to 30 ft (10 m)

Width Up to 20 ft (6 m)

Leaf type Simple

Tree shape Spreading

Location Asia

The American state of Arkansas is famed for its apple orchards. The first apple trees were planted by settlers from farther east in the early 19th century.

Apples contain around 20 percent air.

Apple tree bark peels in thin flakes to reveal lighter brown, new bark beneath.

Five-petaled, the fragrant flower is white with a pink tinge that fades over time.

What **tree** is this?

Does it grow **quickly** or **slowly**?

How **high** does it grow?

What **color** are its leaves in spring?

Where is a popular **place** to see this tree flowering?

Where in the **world** was it first cultivated?

Deciduous
Prunus incisa

Fuji cherry tree

This hardy, slow-growing deciduous Japanese cherry was first cultivated in 1910 from wild trees growing near Mount Fuji on Honshu, the main island of Japan. When introduced into the western world shortly afterward, it became hugely popular, and was widely planted in gardens and parks.

Height Up to 22 ft (7 m)

Width Up to 20ft (6 m)

Leaf type Simple

Tree shape Spreading

Location Japan

Young trees have an upright shape with ascending branches, while older trees are more wide-spreading. The gray-brown, smooth bark cracks in maturity.

Tens of thousands of people visit Yoshinoyama in Japan every year to see 30,000 cherry trees in bloom.

The leaves are bronze-red in spring and fade to green before turning bright red and gold.

Symbol of life

What **tree** is this?

What **shape** are its leaves?

What **year** did it arrive in Britain?

Is the bark **smooth** or **patterned**?

How **long** do its leaves grow?

This tree has been cultivated in **Japan** for over 3,000 years. True or false?

Deciduous
Prunus serrulata

Hill cherry tree

A small, flat-topped tree with spreading branches, the hill cherry is grown as an ornamental tree in botanic gardens. It is believed to be the first cultivated Japanese cherry to be introduced into the West. It arrived in Britain via China in 1822. The species is known to have been cultivated in Japan for at least 1,000 years.

Height Up to 15 ft (5 m)

Width Up to 15 ft (5 m)

Leaf type Simple

Tree shape Spreading

Location China, Japan

In Japan and throughout the world, picnics and parties are held to celebrate the cherry blossom season.

The leaves are roughly oval-shaped, up to 5 in (13 cm) long and 2 in (5 cm) wide, with a long tapered point and a finely serrated margin. Their upper surface is bright green, while the underside is blue-green.

The bark is gray-brown, with a slight sheen and horizontal banding.

Golden fruit

What **tree** is this?

What kind of **musical instruments** are made from its wood?

How many **petals** does its flower have?

What color is the flesh of the **fruit** from this tree?

In which season does this tree **blossom**?

There are around **500 varieties** of this tree. True or false?

Common pear tree

The common pear tree is believed to be a hybrid that originated in western Asia more than 2,000 years ago. It has been cultivated throughout the western world for centuries. Today, there are over 1,000 varieties available commercially, each one with slightly different form, size, fruit, or flowers.

Height Up to 50 ft (15 m)

Width Up to 40 ft (12 m)

Leaf type Simple

Tree shape Varies

Location Asia

The broadly oval leaves are hairy when young, becoming smooth as they mature. They are glossy, dark green above, with a heart-shaped base and pointed tip.

The edible fruit has creamy white flesh, which surrounds hard, brown seeds.

The wood from common pear trees is often used to make woodwind instruments.

The white, five-petaled flowers blossom in spring.

What **tree** is this?

Is it a **large** or **small** tree?

The fruit is **hairy** when young. True or false?

What **color** is its bark?

It is known for **living** a long time. True or false?

What **three** countries is it native to?

Does it have **edible** fruit?

Deciduous
Pyrus salicifolia

Willow-leaved pear tree

This small, weeping tree is also known as the weeping silver-leaved pear tree. The most ornamental of pear trees, it is native to Russia, Turkey, and northern Iraq. Today it is planted in gardens and parks. The willow-leaved pear is not a long-lived tree. Its gray bark becomes cracked with age.

Height Up to 30 ft (10 m)

Width Up to 22 ft (7 m)

Leaf type Simple

Tree shape Weeping

Location Asia, Europe

The fruit is a small, hard pear, up to 1¼ in (3 cm) long. Hairy when young, it turns smooth with age. Mature leaves are light green and smooth.

Unlike other pear trees, the fruit of this tree is inedible.

Velvety soft fruit

What **tree** is this?

Its fruit was a symbol of **luxury**. True or false?

Is it a **large** or **small** tree?

How **wide** does it grow?

Does it have **sweet** or **sour** fruit?

What other **fruit** can also grow on this tree?

Deciduous
Prunus persica

Peach tree

This small, spreading tree has been cultivated for its fruit for centuries. The species name *persica* derives from an early European belief that this tree came from Persia (modern-day Iran). However, botanists now believe that the peach is probably native to China, and was introduced into Persia along trade routes.

Height Up to 30 ft (10 m)

Width 30 ft (10 m)

Leaf type Simple

Tree shape Spreading

Location China

In Chinese literature, peaches were symbols of luxury and privilege, and were often painted on Chinese porcelain.

As nectarines differ from peaches by only one gene, they can grow on peach trees.

The skin of the fruit encloses yellow or whitish flesh, which is sweet and juicy when ripe.

Purple fruit

What **tree** is this?

Does it have **fragrant** flowers?

The seed of the fruit can be **poisonous** if chewed. True or false?

How **high** does it grow?

What is the **seed** of the fruit called?

Plum tree

Also known as garden plum, this small, broadly spreading tree is widely cultivated for its fruit. The tree has a broad and spreading crown. When young, its bark is smooth and has a slight sheen. The leaves, up to 1 in (2.5 cm) wide, have a dull grass-green upper surface and slightly blue-green underside.

Height Up to 30 ft (10 m)

Width Up to 20 ft (6 m)

Leaf type Simple

Tree shape Spreading

Location Europe

The plum stone contains cyanide compounds and can be poisonous if chewed.

The flowers are fragrant, and grow in spring, before leaves appear. The flowers are up to 1 in (2.5 cm) wide.

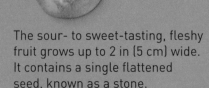

The sour- to sweet-tasting, fleshy fruit grows up to 2 in (5 cm) wide. It contains a single flattened seed, known as a stone.

What **tree** is this?

How many **petals** does its flower have?

The flowers are **dark purple**. True or false?

What is the name of the **coat** covering its fruit?

What part of the tree is **edible**?

Which famous **king** liked the produce from this tree?

Almond tree

This deciduous, spreading tree is known widely for its fruit. When ripe, the flesh of the green fruit separates from the flattened stone, which contains an edible white seed. The gray-black bark is smooth at first, cracking into small squares with age. The five-petaled flowers open before the leaves emerge.

Height 12–30 ft (4–10 m)

Width 20 ft (6 m)

Leaf type Simple

Tree shape Spreading

Location Asia, Africa

This sweet-tasting nut has been a key ingredient in desserts and cakes for centuries. Ground almonds are also used to make many cookies and macarons.

The fruit is covered in a gray-green coat called a hull. Inside, a hard shell contains the edible seed.

Almonds were found in King Tutankhamun's tomb in Egypt.

The five-petaled flowers are white, sometimes faintly pink, and grow singly or in pairs in early spring before the leaves emerge.

Ruby jewels

What **tree** is this?

In ancient **Rome**, newly wed women sometimes wore crowns made from this tree's leaves. True or false?

How did the ancient **Egyptians** use the fruit from this tree?

Which religious **book** mentions the fruit of this tree?

The fruit was a **symbol** of fertility. True or false?

What are the juice **sacs** of the fruit called?

Deciduous
Punica granatum

Pomegranate tree

The pomegranate tree was first cultivated around 5,000 years ago and soon spread throughout the ancient world. To the ancient Egyptians, who often used the fruit as a medicine, the pomegranate was a symbol of fertility and prosperity. Pomegranates are also mentioned many times in the Bible.

Height Up to 25 ft (8 m)

Width Up to 20 ft (6 m)

Leaf type Simple

Tree shape Shrublike

Location Asia, Mediterranean

Pomegranates were known and enjoyed in ancient Rome. In this Roman fresco from the 1st century BCE, birds perch on pomegranate trees.

In ancient Rome, newly wed women sometimes wore crowns woven from pomegranate leaves.

When a pomegranate is opened, hundreds of shiny deep-red juice sacs (arils) are revealed.

What **tree** is this?

How **wide** does it grow?

Where is it often **planted**?

When do male **flowers** appear on this tree?

Where in the **world** is it found?

How much can this tree **grow** in a year?

Deciduous
Salix babylonica

Weeping willow

One of the best-known trees in the temperate world, the weeping willow is commonly planted alongside rivers and lakes. It is a wide-spreading, medium-sized tree with a drooping shape, featuring a wide head of relatively level branches from which long, slender branchlets hang almost vertically.

Height Up to 80 ft (25 m)

Width Up to 50 ft (15 m)

Leaf type Simple

Tree shape Weeping

Location China

The tree has long, hanging yellow shoots. The leaves end in tapered points.

The weeping willow is one of the fastest-growing trees on Earth, growing up to 4 ft (1.2 m) per year.

Male flowers are yellow-green, and appear with young leaves in spring in slender catkins.

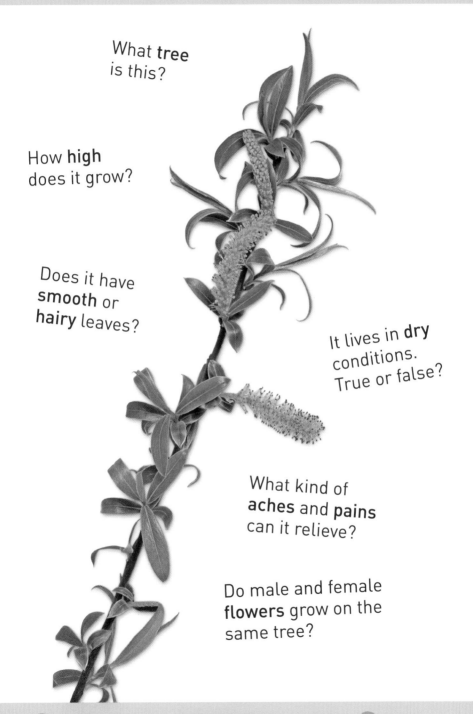

What **tree** is this?

How **high** does it grow?

Does it have **smooth** or **hairy** leaves?

It lives in **dry** conditions. True or false?

What kind of **aches** and **pains** can it relieve?

Do male and female **flowers** grow on the same tree?

Deciduous
Salix alba

White willow

A broadly columnar, medium-sized tree, the white willow thrives in damp soils, and is normally found growing alongside rivers. A dense coating of hairs on the leaves gives this tree a silvery appearance. Young leaves are coated with silver hairs on both sides. Mature leaves retain hairs on the underside.

Height Up to 80 ft (25 m)

Width Up to 70 ft (20 m)

Leaf type Simple

Tree shape Columnar

Location Asia, Europe

The shoots are slender, and light gray-pink to olive-brown.

The white willow was traditionally used as a pain reliever for headaches and toothaches.

Both male and female flowers are clustered in catkins on separate trees. Female flowers become fluffy with white-haired seeds.

Cascading flowers

What **tree** is this?

What **color** are its seeds?

Is it found growing in **mountainous** regions?

It has leaves made up of **two** leaflets. True or false?

Is it **short-** or **long**-lived?

This tree is also called **golden rain**. True or false?

Common laburnum

Probably one of the most familiar trees in cultivation in Europe, the common laburnum is small and broad-spreading. Native to southern and central Europe, it naturally occurs in mountainous regions. It is short-lived—between 50 and 60 years is considered a long age.

Height Up to 28 ft (9 m)

Width Up to 15 ft (5 m)

Leaf type Compound

Tree shape Spreading

Location Europe

The fruits are green, hairy, beanlike seed pods containing several small, round, black seeds.

Common laburnum trees are also called golden rain due to their cascading, yellow flowers.

Each leaf is composed of three leaflets, rich green on the upper surface, gray-green on the underside and covered with silver hairs when young.

What **tree** is this?

Where in the **world** does this tree grow?

It is a **hybrid** of which two trees?

What are its **seeds** called?

When does it **bloom**?

The seeds can be used for making **soap** and **cosmetics**. True or false?

Deciduous
Aesculus x carnea

Red horse chestnut

This tree is a hybrid between the horse chestnut and red buckeye. Its bark is dull brown and smooth when young, developing shallow cracks and breaking into flaking plates with age. The fruit, sometimes covered in spines, splits in segments to reveal up to three seeds (known as conkers in Europe).

Height Up to 70 ft (20 m)

Width Up to 30 ft (10 m)

Leaf type Compound

Tree shape Columnar

Location Germany

The leaflets have parallel veins and are joined at the base to a long, pink-green stalk.

The red horse chestnut seeds are used to make soaps and cosmetics.

The canopy of the large red horse chestnut starts blooming from mid- to late spring.

Champion fruit

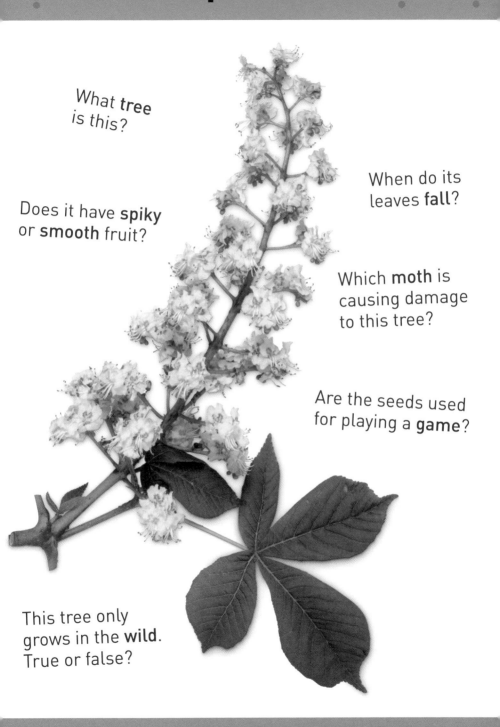

What **tree** is this?

When do its leaves **fall**?

Does it have **spiky** or **smooth** fruit?

Which **moth** is causing damage to this tree?

Are the seeds used for playing a **game**?

This tree only grows in the **wild**. True or false?

Common horse chestnut

One of the most common trees in cultivation, this horse chestnut originated in the Balkans of southeastern Europe. It has recently come under attack from a leaf-mining moth and a bleeding canker bacterium, both of which are causing damage to trees across Europe.

Height Up to 100 ft (30 m)

Width Up to 50 ft (15 m)

Leaf type Compound

Tree shape Columnar

Location Greece, Albania

The bark is gray to brown-orange and smooth, becoming shallowly cracked and scaly in maturity.

The fruit is a rounded green husk with spikes and measures up to 2½ in (6 cm) wide. It contains one to three shiny red-brown seeds known as conkers.

Leaves with up to seven leaflets, each up to 10 in (25 cm) long, turn golden brown before falling in mid-autumn.

The conkers are used in a game where players try to crack their opponents' conkers with their own.

What **tree** is this?

The fruit of this tree is used to treat illnesses in which **animal**?

What **color** are its young leaves?

Does it grow in the **mountains**?

It has **upright** flower clusters. True or false?

Does it have **rough** or **smooth** bark?

Deciduous
Aesculus indica

Indian horse chestnut

This large, broadly columnar tree is native to north India and the northwest Himalayas, where it grows in the foothills up to 9,840 ft (3,000 m) above sea level. It is planted in parks and gardens across the world, especially Europe and North America. The bark is gray-brown and smooth, even in maturity.

Height 80–100 ft (25–30 m)

Width Up to 40 ft (12 m)

Leaf type Compound

Tree shape Columnar

Location India, Himalayas

Bronze-colored leaflets emerge in spring, turning glossy grass green in summer and yellow in the fall.

The slender, white to pale pink flowers develop on upright clusters up to 10 in (25 cm) long.

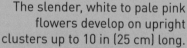

The fruits of the Indian horse chestnut have been used to treat some health conditions in horses.

Goblet-shaped flower

What **tree** is this?

How **wide** does it grow?

Are the leaves **smooth** or **hairy** on the top?

What **color** is the ripe fruit?

This tree is **common** in the wild. True or false?

Who **created** this tree?

Deciduous
Magnolia x soulangeana

Saucer magnolia

This tree was the first hybrid magnolia and does not occur in the wild. Raised near Paris in the 1820s, today it is the world's most widely planted garden magnolia. It tends to have multiple stems with low branches. The bark is smooth and gray, while flowers vary from creamy white to pink or purple-pink.

Height 25–40 ft (8–12 m)

Width Up to 30 ft (10 m)

Leaf type Simple

Tree shape Spreading

Location Originated in Europe

The leaves are smooth and dark green on the upper surface, and paler and finely hairy on the underside.

The saucer magnolia was created by Étienne Soulange-Bodin, a retired officer from Napoleon's army.

The fruit is an irregular cylindrical cluster, ripening from green to pink-red.

What **tree** is this?

What year was it **discovered**?

How **high** does it grow?

Where in the **world** does this tree grow?

What does the **fruit** of this tree look like?

Which part of Canada has this tree on its **coat of arms**?

Deciduous
Cornus nuttallii

Pacific dogwood

With a natural habitat ranging from British Columbia to California, the Pacific dogwood has been cultivated outside this region since its discovery in 1835. In cultivation, this tree rarely achieves its full height, often growing as a large, multistemmed shrub or small tree up to 30 ft (10 m) tall.

Height 80 ft (25 m)

Width Up to 50 ft (15 m)

Leaf type Simple

Tree shape Varies

Location North America

In late spring, flowers appear in dense clusters, up to 1 in (2.5 cm) wide, followed by small, red fruit.

The leaves turn yellow or red in autumn before falling.

The Pacific dogwood is British Columbia's floral emblem and appears on its coat of arms.

The fruit is rounded and strawberrylike, and grows on long stalks.

Fluffy pods

This flower grows on what type of **tree**?

The pods from this tree resemble what **fluffy material**?

Does it grow **quickly** or **slowly**?

Are the flowers **tiny**?

Does it have a **thorny** trunk?

What color **seeds** does it have?

Deciduous
Chorisia speciosa

Silk floss tree

Native to South America, the silk floss tree is cultivated elsewhere as an ornamental tree in parks and gardens. This fast-growing, broadly spreading, medium-sized tree is attractive while in flower. The tree is related to the kapok and African baobab.

Height Up to 70 ft (20 m)

Width Up to 70 ft (20 m)

Leaf type Compound

Tree shape Spreading

Location South America

Hibiscus-like flowers emerge from bulging green buds from spring into summer, and grow up to 6 in (15 cm) wide.

The pods contain black seeds surrounded by fluffy material resembling sheep's wool.

The trunk is covered with conical thorns to prevent animals from climbing the tree.

The leaves are up to 10 in (25 cm) wide, and consist of five to seven leaflets, each up to 5 in (12 cm) long.

What **tree** is this?

It was believed to protect against **evil spirits**. True or false?

Does it grow in the **mountains**?

What **shape** does it form?

Is it a **weak** or **hardy** tree?

Which **Norse god** was believed to have been saved by this tree?

Deciduous
Sorbus aucuparia

Rowan

This conical, deciduous tree can grow up to 3,280 ft (1,000 m) above sea level in mountainous regions. It is a particularly hardy tree and its berries are an important food source for birds. In some regions of Europe, a rowan tree planted outside the house is considered protection against evil spirits.

Height Up to 70 ft (20 m)

Width Up to 22 ft (7 m)

Leaf type Compound

Tree shape Conical

Location Asia, Europe

The fruit appears toward the end of summer on stalks up to ¾ in (2 cm) long and remains on the tree until eaten by birds.

In Norse mythology, a rowan tree saved the god Thor from being swept away in a river of the Underworld.

The flowers are fragrant and develop in dense clusters, up to 6 in (15 cm) wide, in late spring.

Black buds

Is it a **large** or **small** tree?

What **tree** is this?

What time of year does it **flower**?

Does it **spread** easily?

Is this tree in the **rose** family?

What **color** is its bark when young?

It often has a **crooked** trunk. True or false?

Deciduous
Fraxinus excelsior

Common ash

This broadly columnar tree is one of the largest European deciduous trees. It is common in woods, field boundaries, and open wetlands. It has become invasive in some urban areas, seeding itself with ease into gardens and parks. It has a light, airy crown and a trunk that tends to be straight.

Height Up to 130 ft (40 m)

Width Up to 70 ft (20 m)

Leaf type Compound

Tree shape Columnar

Location Europe

Ash trees produce oil that scientists think could be a good source of nutritional compounds.

Flowers appear in late winter, clustered along the previous year's shoots.

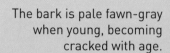

The bark is pale fawn-gray when young, becoming cracked with age.

Sweet sap

How **wide** does it grow?

What **tree** is this?

What **color** do the leaves turn in the fall?

Which **sweetener** is made from the sap of this tree?

Does the fruit of this tree hang in **clusters**?

Are the leaves **matte** or **shiny** on the upper side?

Manna ash

This medium-sized tree has been widely cultivated in parks and gardens throughout Europe since before 1700. Unlike most ash trees, manna ash produces large panicles (branching clusters) of creamy white, fragrant flowers. Mannitol, a medicine and sweetener, comes from the tree's sap.

Height Up to 70 ft (20 m)

Width Up to 50 ft (15 m)

Leaf type Compound

Tree shape Spreading

Location Asia, Europe

Matte green on the upper surface, the leaflets have a pale green underside. In autumn, they turn bright yellow before falling.

Manna ash sap is collected as a pale yellow gum that dries on contact with air.

Fruit develops in long, hanging clusters and remains on the tree late into the fall.

Highly prized

What **tree** is this?

Does it grow **quickly** or **slowly**?

Are the seeds of this tree **edible**?

What **color** are its leaves when young?

In which of the **seven wonders** of the Ancient World did this tree grow?

Who **introduced** this tree to Britain?

Deciduous
Juglans regia

Common walnut

This slow-growing tree has been widely cultivated for its nuts and highly prized decorative lumber since the Roman Empire. The Romans introduced it to the British Isles. Today, it can be found in seminatural forests from China through Central Asia to southern Europe; it is cultivated in northern Europe, the Americas, Australia and New Zealand, and elsewhere.

Height Up to 100 ft (30 m)

Width Up to 50 ft (15 m)

Leaf type Compound

Tree shape Spreading

Location Asia, Europe

Walnuts were said to have grown in the Hanging Gardens of Babylon, one of the seven wonders of the Ancient World.

Its aromatic leaves are pink-bronze when young. They consist of up to nine leaflets, growing from a main leaf stalk.

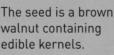

The seed is a brown walnut containing edible kernels.

What **tree** is this?

What **color** are the male catkins when ripe?

Where in the **world** does it grow?

What type of **oil** was produced from this tree in the past?

Do male and female flowers grow on **separate** trees?

What shape are its **nuts**?

Bitternut hickory

This large tree is native to southeastern United States. It is planted elsewhere in parks and gardens for its fall leaf color and ornamental ridged, gray bark. Its fruits are hard nuts that are unpleasant to eat. They do, however, have a high oil content, and were once crushed to produce lamp oil.

Height Up to 100 ft (30 m)

Width Up to 50 ft (15 m)

Leaf type Compound

Tree shape Columnar

Location United States

Leaves are deep green on the upper surface and yellow-green on the underside. They turn golden yellow in the fall.

Both male and female flowers are carried on separate catkins on the same tree in late spring. Male catkins ripen from green to gold.

The bitternut hickory's Latin name, cordiformis, meaning "heart-shaped", refers to the shape of the nuts.

Sturdy survivor

What **tree** is this?

What **shape** does it form?

How **high** can it grow?

Which **insect** does its seed pod look like?

Why is it planted in **cities**?

Does it have **smooth** or **spiny** bark?

Honey locust

The honey locust tree is often identified by its prickly thorns, which cover its trunk and main branches. It is widely planted in city streets because of its tolerance to heat, dust, drought, and airborne pollutants. Unlike other trees of the pea family, it does not produce the "wing and keel" pea flower.

Height 70–100 ft (20–30 m)

Width Up to 70 ft (20 m)

Leaf type Compound

Tree shape Spreading

Location United States

The seed-bearing fruit is a large, twisted, hanging pod up to 18 in (45 cm) long. Green at first, it ripens to olive-brown.

The name honey locust comes from the seed pods, which look like locusts and contain a sweet substance.

The bark is gray-brown, and smooth when young, developing clusters of sharp spines in maturity.

Bird magnet

What **tree** is this?

Is it a **small** or **large** tree?

What other tree is it **related** to?

Which **bird** feeds from its flowers?

What color **bark** does it have?

Does it have **yellow-pink** or **green-blue** leaf stalks?

Where in the **world** does it grow?

Deciduous
Aesculus pavia

Red buckeye

Sometimes no more than a large shrub, this small tree grows in moist woods and thickets. The red buckeye is one of the parents of the red horse chestnut and gives the red coloring to its flowers. Its dark gray bark is smooth at first and cracks into irregular plates with age.

Height Up to 22 ft (7 m)

Width Up to 10 ft (3 m)

Leaf type Compound

Tree shape Varies

Location United States

The pear-shaped fruit is a golden, russet-green, ripening to light brown. It appears after the flowers.

Each leaflet is carried on a yellow-pink petiole (leaf stalk) up to 7 in (18 cm) long. In the fall, the leaves turn orange and red.

The nectar-rich flowers of the red buckeye often attract hummingbirds.

Trumpet-shaped flower

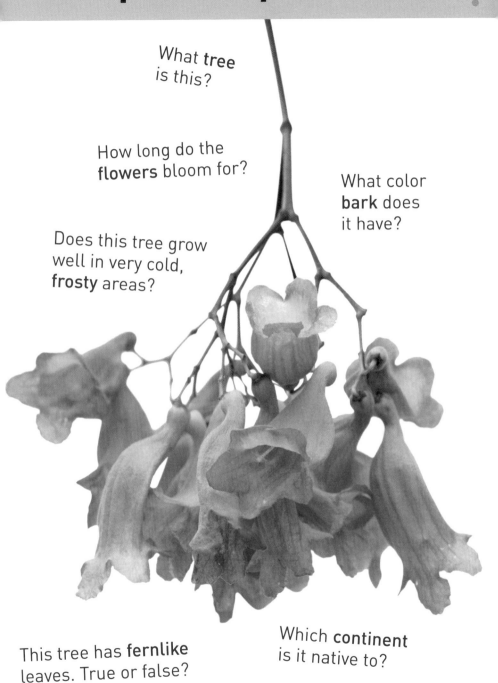

What **tree** is this?

How long do the **flowers** bloom for?

What color **bark** does it have?

Does this tree grow well in very cold, **frosty** areas?

This tree has **fernlike** leaves. True or false?

Which **continent** is it native to?

Deciduous
Jacaranda mimosifolia

Jacaranda

The jacaranda is native to South America, but it has been cultivated in almost every part of the world where there is no risk of frost. It is known for its beautiful, long-lasting flowers and fernlike leaves. Birds, bees, and insects are attracted to the tree during its flowering season.

Height Up to 50 ft (15 m)

Width Up to 50 ft (15 m)

Leaf type Compound

Tree shape Spreading

Location South America

The leaves are fernlike, with a maximum of 20 pairs of pinnae (leaf divisions), each carrying up to 28 pairs of bright green ½ in- (1 cm-) long leaflets.

Pretoria, South Africa, is nicknamed the Jacaranda City, and is home to rare white jacarandas.

The mature tree produces a striking mass of lilac-blue flowers, which last for around two months.

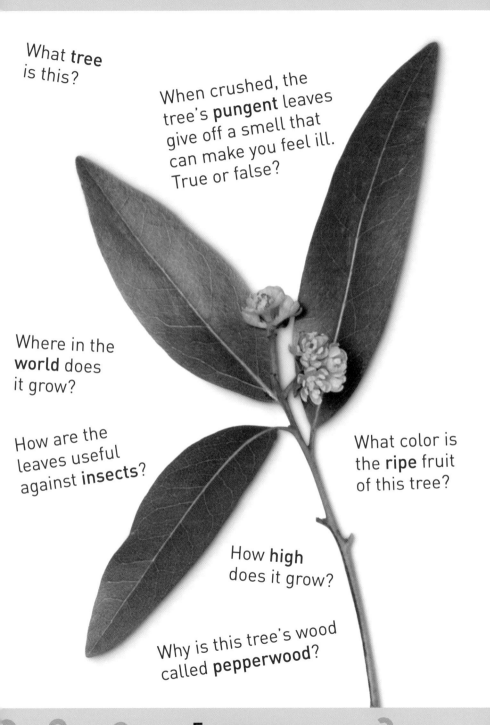

What **tree** is this?

When crushed, the tree's **pungent** leaves give off a smell that can make you feel ill. True or false?

Where in the **world** does it grow?

How are the leaves useful against **insects**?

What color is the **ripe** fruit of this tree?

How **high** does it grow?

Why is this tree's wood called **pepperwood**?

Evergreens
Umbellularia californica

California laurel

Also known as the California bay, California olive, and Oregon myrtle, this is a vigorous, dense, leafy tree. The foliage, when crushed, emits a strong odor, which can cause nausea and headaches. Its highly prized lumber, known as pepperwood because of the strong-smelling leaves, ranges in color from blonde, like maple, to a dark wood that is similar to walnut.

Height 80–100 ft (25–30 m)

Width Up to 30 ft (10 m)

Leaf type Simple

Tree shape Shrublike

Location United States

The leaves, which are carried on sage-green shoots, are glossy bright green on the upper surface and yellow-green on the underside.

Flowers are followed by small, pear-shaped berries ripening from green to dark purple.

Smoke from burning California laurel leaves is used as an insect repellent.

What **tree** is this?

Can it be grown as a **hedge**?

Where in the **world** does it grow?

It is too **dense** to be clipped into architectural forms. True or false?

Are the small flowers **scented**?

It is used to **decorate** homes and churches. True or false?

Portuguese laurel

A small to medium-sized tree, the Portuguese laurel is taller in its natural habitat. It is quite often clipped into architectural forms and grown as a dense, luxuriant hedge or screen. It has been cultivated in this way since the 17th century, or even earlier. The bark is slate-gray to gray-brown.

Height Up to 30 ft (10 m)

Width Up to 30 ft (10 m)

Leaf type Simple

Tree shape Shrublike

Location Europe

The evergreen Portuguese laurel is shrubby and multistemmed, and serves well as a hedge or screen.

In Portugal, people decorate their homes and churches with Portuguese laurel at Easter and Christmas.

Long clusters of fruit follow the scented creamy white flowers, which look like lily of the valley. The individual fruits are widely spaced along the stalk.

What **tree** is this?

What **shape** does it form?

Does it have **rough** or **smooth** bark?

How is it used in **cooking**?

The ancient Greeks and Romans used the leaves to make **crowns**. True or false?

The berries grow on **male** trees. True or false?

Bay laurel

This densely leaved tree has a distinguished history dating back to ancient times. It is native to the Mediterranean region but is now more widely planted for ornamental and hedging purposes. It is a multistemmed tree with bark that remains smooth even in old age. The leaves of bay laurel are dark green and leathery.

Height 20–60 ft (6–18 m)

Width Up to 30 ft (10 m)

Leaf type Simple

Tree shape Conical

Location Mediterranean

Male and female flowers grow on separate trees in late winter, followed by berries on female trees.

The fragrant leaves of bay laurel can be used to add flavor to food.

The Greeks and Romans used bay laurel as a symbol of victory, weaving it into crowns to be worn by champions.

What **tree** is this?

Does it grow **quickly** or **slowly**?

Does it grow **apple-shaped** fruit?

What is its fruit called in **South Africa**?

Is the trunk of this tree **hard** or **soft**?

Papaya tree

This fast-growing, short-lived evergreen is native to Central and South America but is also grown elsewhere for its juicy, edible fruit. Although it looks like a tree, the papaya is not strictly a tree but a herbaceous plant. The trunk does not lay down wood, as in a normal tree, and always remains soft.

Height Up to 22 ft (7 m)

Width Up to 12 ft (4 m)

Leaf type Simple

Tree shape Columnar

Location Central and South America

The flowers are cream to greenish-white in color, and develop into a pear-shaped fruit.

Papaya plants can produce fruit in their first year.

The fruit, also known as pawpaw in South Africa, hangs in clumps below the branches. When ripe, a papaya has a thin, greenish-yellow skin and pinkish-orange, sweet-tasting flesh.

What **tree** is this?

The ripe fruit of this tree is **green**. True or false?

How is the fruit of this tree often **eaten**?

Is it the **smallest** or **largest** cultivated fruit tree?

Is this tree often depicted in **art**?

Where in the **world** does it grow?

The **oldest** tree is 100 years old. True or false?

Evergreens
Mangifera indica

Mango tree

Native to India, the mango tree has been widely cultivated throughout the tropics for millennia. It was grown in East Asia as early as 500 BCE. Today, it is probably the best known and most popular of all tropical fruit and is regularly eaten worldwide. Mango trees are also a popular motif in art, culture, and literature around the world.

Height 100 ft (30 m)

Width 50 ft (15 m)

Leaf type Simple

Tree shape Varies

Location Asia

The largest cultivated fruit tree, the mango has a trunk that carries a dense crown of dark green leaves.

The size of the fruit is variable, but normally similar to that of the avocado. It ripens to yellow, orange, or red.

The oldest mango tree, located in India, is 300 years old and still produces fruit.

One of the ways in which mangoes are eaten is in chutney, an accompaniment to many Indian dishes.

Sweet treat

What **tree** is this?

What product is made from the **beans** of this tree?

The flowers of this tree grow out of the **trunk**. True or false?

What does the **Latin name** of this tree mean?

Are the fruits from this tree shaped like **footballs**?

Which **insect** plays a key role in helping to pollinate the flowers?

Cacao tree

This small tree provides cocoa—the key ingredient of chocolate. The name chocolate comes from the Aztec word *xocolatl*, which means "bitter water." The cacao tree is indigenous to Central America, but has been widely cultivated in the Caribbean, Africa, Java, and Sri Lanka for its cocoa seeds, which are roasted and ground to make cocoa powder and chocolate.

Height Up to 30 ft (10 m)

Width Up to 25 ft (8 m)

Leaf type Simple

Tree shape Spreading

Location Central America

The creamy yellow to pink flowers emerge directly from the trunk and main branches. These flowers are so small that they can only be pollinated by tiny midges.

The Latin name of the cacao tree, *Theobroma*, means "food of the gods."

The pod-shaped fruit looks like footballs. When the seeds are removed from gooey pulp inside the pod and roasted, they change color from white to brown and are called cocoa beans.

What **tree** is this?

Can its **fruit** be eaten?

Items carved from its wood have been found in ancient Egyptian **tombs**. True or false?

Why did Indian **kings** drink from cups made from this wood?

Where in the **world** does it grow?

What color is the tree's **heartwood**?

Ebony

There are several trees with the commercial name ebony, but this species—with its dense black, extremely hard heartwood—is the best known. It is native to southern India and Sri Lanka. Ebony, which has a variety of uses, has been valued since ancient times for its black wood—carved ebony items have even been found in ancient Egyptian tombs.

Height 70–80 ft (20–25 m)

Width Up to 70 ft (20 m)

Leaf type Simple

Tree shape Spreading

Location India, Sri Lanka

Ancient Indian kings drank from ebony cups because they believed it could neutralize poison.

The female flowers are followed by the fruit, which is an edible rounded berry, similar in appearance to a small persimmon. It is ¾ in (2 cm) wide, and green when young.

Strangler tree

What **tree** is this?

This tree is the **national tree** of which country?

What **animal** helps this tree to spread?

Does this tree have **aerial** roots?

Does it have a **dense** or **light** canopy?

One of these trees has a crown circumference of **1¼ miles**. True or false?

What color is the **ripe** fruit of this tree?

Banyan

Like other fig trees, banyans are stranglers—starting life as a seed deposited by a bird among the branches of another tree. This seed develops aerial roots that grow down to the ground and thicken once they reach the soil. They eventually strangle the host tree. The canopy of this tree casts a dense shade.

Height 70–80 ft (20–25 m)

Width Up to 70 ft (20 m)

Leaf type Simple

Tree shape Spreading

Location India

A banyan in the botanic garden near Kolkata in India has a crown circumference of about 0.6 miles (1 km). It is more than 250 years old.

The fruit is a round fig, up to ¾ in (2 cm) wide. It is green and ripens to scarlet.

The banyan is the national tree of India.

Useful bark

What **tree** is this?

How long can this tree **live** for?

What is the **fruit** called?

Does it have **spongy** bark?

Where in the **world** does it grow?

How is the outer **bark** used?

Cork oak

The cork oak is native to the western Mediterranean region, northern Africa, and the southern European Atlantic coast. It has been widely cultivated over many centuries for its thick, spongy bark called cork, which has been used to make cork products, including bottle stoppers and sporting equipment.

Height Up to 70 ft (20 m)

Width 70 ft (20 m)

Leaf type Simple

Tree shape Spreading

Location Africa, Europe

The oak's seeds are found in fruits called acorns. They are green ripening to brown, and encased for half its length in a scaly cup. It is up to 1¼ in (3 cm) long.

A cork oak tree can live for 200 years, yielding 20 crops of cork over that time.

Once every ten years or so, in managed cork oakwoods, the dead outer bark is stripped off the trunks in large slabs, but the cork grows back.

What **tree** is this?

The male and female catkins grow on **separate** trees. True or false?

Does it have a **dense** canopy?

What **color** is its bark?

What colour are the male **catkins**?

What are the **ancient Greeks** thought to have used the leaves of this tree for?

Evergreens
Quercus ilex

Holm oak

The holm oak has a rounded, domed shape, and dense branching. Its foliage makes the canopy look solid and black from a distance. Little light or rainwater filters through the canopy to ground level, so the ground beneath this tree is normally bare, except for dry, brown, spent leaves.

Height Up to 100 ft (30 m)

Width Up to 100 ft (30 m)

Leaf type Simple

Tree shape Spreading

Location Europe, Mediterranean

The bark is gray-brown and smooth. It develops shallow fissures (cracks) and small plates with age.

In ancient Greece, the leaves of the holm oak were thought to reveal the future.

The male and female catkins appear separately on the same tree in summer. Male catkins are creamy gray.

What **tree** is this?

Which **rainforest** is this tree native to?

Which **disease** can it help treat?

The glossy green leaves are eaten by **caterpillars**. True or false?

Are its flowers **smooth** or **hairy**?

Does it have **fragrant** flowers?

How **high** does it grow?

Quinine tree

This tree is native to the Amazon rainforest. Its discovery led to one of the most important medical advancements in human history. The bark of the quinine tree and related *Cinchona* species is the only known natural source of quinine, a chemical compound that is an effective treatment for malaria.

Height 50 ft (15 m)

Width Up to 30 ft (10 m)

Leaf type Simple

Tree shape Spreading

Location South America

Caterpillars dislike the taste of quinine, and won't eat the leaves of the tree.

The small, fragrant flower grows at the tip of open-stalked panicles. Both the flowers and the panicles are covered in fine, silvery-white hairs.

What **tree** is this?

Does it grow **quickly** or **slowly**?

Is this tree **hardy** or **tender**?

The young leaves are **pointed**. True or false?

Which **country** is it native to?

The **oil** extracted from the leaves cannot be used in medicine. True or false?

Does it have **flaky** bark?

Evergreens
Eucalyptus gunnii

Cider gum

This fast-growing tree is native to Tasmania, where it grows in moist mountain forests up to 4,265 ft (1,300 m) above sea level. One of the hardiest of all *Eucalyptus* species, it is widely planted in temperate regions as an ornamental tree and for lumber. The foliage is often used in flower arrangements.

Height Up to 100 ft (30 m)

Width Up to 50 ft (15 m)

Leaf type Simple

Tree shape Columnar

Location South Australia, Tasmania

The bark is mottled gray-green and copper. It flakes in long strips to reveal a cream surface below.

The leaves of the cider gum contain eucalyptus oil, which is used in medicines and cosmetics.

The young leaves are rounded. They are virtually stalkless, and are carried in opposite pairs on shoots.

What **tree** is this?

What other **name** is it called?

How **high** does it grow?

Is it a **fast-growing** tree?

This tree thrives in **mountain** forests. True or false?

It has **egg-shaped** fruit. True or false?

Tasmanian snow gum

This large tree is one of the hardiest and most attractive of the eucalyptus trees. In Tasmania it grows in the central mountain ranges up to 4,590 ft (1,400 m) above sea level. A spreading, fast-growing species, it was first introduced into Britain around 1840, and has been widely planted across Europe since then.

Height Up to 80 ft (25 m)

Width Up to 25 ft (8 m)

Leaf type Simple

Tree shape Spreading

Location Tasmania

The bark is smooth and mottled gray-white. It peels in vertical strips to reveal a creamy white layer.

The fruit is a green, woody, funnel-shaped capsule that contains several seeds. It ripens to gray-brown.

There are around 750 eucalyptus species—mostly native to Australia.

Prized nectar

What **tree** is this?

How many **petals** do its flowers have?

What **shape** does it form?

What **color** are its flower stamens?

It grows in the **Atlas mountains**. True or false?

What have scientists discovered about the **honey** made from the nectar of this tree?

Ulmo

This elegant tree grows in the foothills of the Andes mountain range, at an altitude of up to 2,300 ft (700 m) above sea level. It was first cultivated in Europe around 1851. In its native Chile and Argentina, it is currently threatened by logging and loss of habitat. This densely branched tree is conical.

Height 30–70 ft (10–20 m)

Width Up to 25 ft (8 m)

Leaf type Simple

Tree shape Conical

Location Chile, Argentina

Honey made from the nectar of ulmo flowers has been scientifically proven to help wounds heal.

Four-petaled flowers appear in late summer. Purple-tipped stamens give the center of the flowers a speckled appearance. Bees collect the flowers' rich nectar, turning it into honey.

What **tree** is this?

It is native to the west coast of **North America**. True or false?

What **shape** does it form?

Does it have **pearlike** fruit?

It grows **taller** in cultivation than in the wild. True or false?

Where in the **world** does it grow?

Evergreens
Arbutus menziesii

Madrone

This tree is called the Pacific or Californian madrone. It grows up to 130 ft (40 m) in the wild, though it normally remains around half this height in cultivation. It is native to the west coast of North America, from British Columbia, including Vancouver Island, Canada, south to California.

Height Up to 130 ft (40 m)

Width Up to 25 ft (8 m)

Leaf type Simple

Tree shape Columnar

Location North America

The fruit is rounded and strawberrylike, and changes from green to orange to red in early fall.

It is widely planted in parks and gardens across the northern temperate world.

The name of the madrone tree comes from the Spanish word Madroño, meaning "strawberry tree."

Strawberrylike fruit

What **tree** is this?

What do people **make** from the berries?

Is the bark **rough** or **smooth**?

What color is the **ripe** fruit?

This is the national tree of **Italy**. True or false?

When do the **flowers** appear?

Killarney strawberry tree

This tree is native to Europe and the Mediterranean, and is the national tree of Italy. It is very popular for hedging in Killarney, Ireland. Young bark is a rich, red-brown color, which fades to a deep brown, and turns rough and fissured. This gives the tree a gnarled appearance. The foliage is glossy green and the fruit look like strawberries.

Height Up to 30 ft (10 m)

Width Up to 12 ft (4 m)

Leaf type Simple

Tree shape Spreading

Location Europe, Mediterranean

The berry is green ripening to red. Though the fruit is edible, it tastes dry and is not particularly enjoyable.

The berries can be cooked to make jellies and preserves.

The flowers appear at the ends of shoots in the fall. They are creamy white and grow in drooping clusters.

What **tree** is this?

Which **animals** eat the fruit from this tree?

Can it grow by the **coast**?

Is it **hardy** or **tender**?

Can its leaves **change** shape?

The male and female **flowers** grow on the same tree. True or false?

Evergreens
Ilex aquifolium

Common holly

With its evergreen leaves and bright red berries, holly's colors are strongly associated with Christmas in the western world, and its branches are used in festive decorations. An extremely hardy tree, it provides shelter for animals in exposed mountainous and coastal locations. Holly is also considerably varied—some even have bright yellow berries instead of red ones.

Height Up to 70 ft (20 m)

Width Up to 50 ft (15 m)

Leaf type Simple

Tree shape Columnar

Location Asia, Africa, Europe

Although the berries are slightly toxic to humans, the fruit is an important source of food for birds and small mammals during the winter months.

Holly tree leaves can adapt and become spikier to deter hungry animals.

Male and female flowers grow on separate trees. Some leaves bear sharp spines, but others are smooth.

What **tree** is this?

This tree is native to **China**. True or false?

Does it have **straight** or **crooked** branches?

Do the berries appear in **spring**?

Who **introduced** it into western cultivation?

Its leaves have more than **10 spines** each. True or false?

Perny's holly

This narrowly conical tree, sometimes large shrub, is native to central and western China. It was introduced into western cultivation by Abbé Paul Perny, a French Jesuit missionary. Today, it is commonly planted in botanical gardens. The branches are straight, ascending, and then arching.

Height Up to 30 ft (10 m)

Width Up to 20 ft (6 m)

Leaf type Simple

Tree shape Varies

Location China

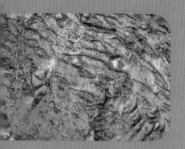

The bark is slate-gray and smooth.

The diamond-shaped leaves, which grow on thick, leathery stalks, are deep glossy green on the upper surface and paler on the underside.

The fruit is a red berry, carried on upright shoots. Appearing in the fall, it persists on the tree well into winter.

Each leaf on the Perny's holly tree has three to seven sharp spines.

Delicious oil

What **tree** is this?

On which Greek island is the **oldest** specimen found?

What **shape** does it form?

Does this tree have a **long** or **short** trunk?

What does the branch **symbolize** in many cultures?

It is **cultivated** for its edible fruit and flavorful oil. True or false?

Olive tree

The olive tree has been highly prized for its fruit and oil for at least 5,000 years. It is also featured in many myths. In Greek mythology, the goddess of war and wisdom, Athena, presented the people of a city with an olive tree, and so Athens was born. An olive branch has also become a symbol of peace across many cultures.

Height Up to 30 ft (10 m)

Width Up to 25 ft (8 m)

Leaf type Simple

Tree shape Spreading

Location Asia, Africa, Europe

The olive tree has a short trunk, which becomes deformed, thick, and hollow with age. Its broadly spreading crown provides welcome shade in hot climates.

A staple of Mediterranean cuisine from ancient times to the present, olive oil is used across the world, for both its health-giving properties and its taste.

The oldest producing olive tree, located in Crete, is thought to be over 4,000 years old.

The fruit is oval, green, and edible. It ripens to glossy purple-black.

What **tree** is this?

Does its bark always feel **warm** or **cold**?

This tree has an unusual bark that is **bright red**. True or false?

Does it like **dry** weather?

Is it grown as a **bonsai** tree?

What color is its fruit when **ripe**?

Evergreens
Luma apiculata

Chilean myrtle

Formerly known by the botanical name *Myrtus luma*, the Chilean myrtle is one of the most interesting trees for bark color. It easily establishes itself in new locations, especially in western Europe, where the North Atlantic Current provides the warm, wet weather it enjoys. The fruit turns purple-black when ripe.

Height Up to 40 ft (12 m)

Width Up to 12 ft (4 m)

Leaf type Simple

Tree shape Columnar

Location Chile, Argentina

The Chilean myrtle is also popular as a bonsai tree.

The tree has a broadly columnar habit. Curiously, its bark feels cold even when in full sunlight. Bright cinnamon-orange with a soft, feltlike texture, it peels in patches to reveal a cream-colored surface beneath.

What **tree** is this?

What other **name** is it called by?

What **shape** does it form?

How **high** does it grow?

Is this tree **hardy** or **tender**?

Who **introduced** this tree into Europe?

The fibrous leaves are used to make **rope**. True or false?

Evergreens
Trachycarpus fortunei

Chusan palm

Also known as the windmill palm, this tree is not indigenous to the tropics, but originates from the mountains of central China. It is a hardy species and can also grow in warmer regions of Europe and North America. It was introduced into Europe by the German physician Philipp Franz von Siebold.

Height Up to 40 ft (12 m)

Width Up to 10 ft (3 m)

Leaf type Compound

Tree shape Columnar

Location China

The fan-shaped leaves are divided almost to the base into about 40 linear, pointed strips. The leaves are attached to the slender trunk by a stiff, flattened leaf stalk.

This palm has a small head of clustered leaves at the top of a single trunk, which is narrower at the base.

In Japan and China, people make cloth and ropes from the fibers of the Chusan palm.

Swordlike leaves

What **tree** is this?

Where in the **world** does it grow?

What succulent plant is it **related** to?

What **color** is its bark?

It has **spongy** bark. True or false?

Does it have **drooping** branches?

Cabbage palm

This palmlike tree is not a true palm, but is more closely related to a succulent plant known as the agave. The cabbage palm tree is native to New Zealand, where the indigenous Māori people used to eat the tender tips of its shoots, hence its common name, "cabbage." It was introduced into Europe in 1823.

Height Up to 30 ft (10 m)

Width Up to 15 ft (5 m)

Leaf type Simple

Tree shape Columnar

Location New Zealand

The cabbage palm bears stout, upright branches, which are crowned by a mass of swordlike leaves.

The bark is gray, corky, and spongy.

The cabbage palm is one of the few New Zealand forest trees that can recover from a fire.

Popular palm

What **tree** is this?

Does the seed contain **edible** white flesh?

Every part of this tree is **useful**. True or false?

The start of the **fishing** season in India is celebrated by offering its fruit. True or false?

What is this tree called in **Malaysia**?

Is its trunk **short** or **long**?

Evergreens
Cocos nucifera

213

Coconut tree

The origin of this popular palm remains a mystery. Some believe it is native to the Pacific and Indian Ocean islands, while others suggest it was introduced from northwest South America. Fossils from around 40 million years ago place it in Australia and India. However, it is now widely spread across the tropics.

Height 70–100 ft (20–30 m)

Width Up to 30 ft (10 m)

Leaf type Compound

Tree shape Columnar

Location Asia, Oceania, the Americas

In Malaysia the coconut palm is called the "tree of a thousand uses" because almost every part of this tree is useful. Utensils, such as this cup, can be carved from coconut shells.

The coconut seeds are hidden inside the fruit. They contain the edible white flesh and coconut milk.

In some parts of India, fishermen celebrate the new fishing season by offering coconuts to the sea.

The trunk is long, slender, and often curving, with a gray bark marked with narrow leaf scars.

Supersized fruit

What **tree** is this?

Is it a **slow-growing** tree?

Does the fruit **taste** sour or sweet?

Where in the **world** does it grow?

Its fruit has a **delicious** smell. True or false?

How much can the fruit **weigh**?

Jackfruit tree

This tree is believed to have originated from southern India, but has been so widely cultivated throughout Asia that it is now difficult to pinpoint its natural range. The jackfruit tree is fast-growing, columnar, and medium-sized. It is cultivated for its edible, fleshy fruit.

Height Up to 70 ft (20 m)

Width Up to 70 ft (20 m)

Leaf type Simple

Tree shape Columnar

Location Asia

The fruit has waxy flesh inside, which may be pink or golden yellow with a strong, unpleasant odor, but tastes like sour banana. The jackfruit flesh is a nutritious carbohydrate used in many dishes, from custards to curries.

Jackfruits are the largest fruits that grow on trees and can weigh up to 100 lb (45 kg).

What **tree** is this?

How **high** does it grow?

What **color** fruit does it have?

A single tree can **produce** up to 500 fruit every season. True or false?

What does its fruit **taste** like when cooked?

Does it have **dull** or **shiny** leaves?

Evergreens
Artocarpus altilis

Breadfruit tree

This fast-growing tree is native to Malaysia, Indonesia, and the Pacific Ocean Islands. However, it has been cultivated in other parts of the tropics for centuries. Broadly columnar, it has ascending, arching branches and a dense crown of foliage. When cooked, its fruit tastes like freshly baked bread.

Height Up to 80 ft (25 m)

Width Up to 70 ft (20 m)

Leaf type Simple

Tree shape Columnar

Location Asia, Pacific Ocean Islands

The fruit weighs up to 11 lb (5 kg). Its green outer skin has hexagon-shaped discs. Inside, the milky flesh looks similar to a melon's. It is the traditional crop in many tropical regions.

The rough, ovate leaves are deep glossy green on the upper surface, and paler on the underside.

A breadfruit tree can produce up to 200 fruit every season.

Ancient fern

What **tree** is this?

Is it **hardy** or **tender**?

It was introduced in **Europe** in the late 1800s. True or false?

In which **season** do new fronds unfurl?

It is **not really** a tree at all. True or false?

Is the bark **fibrous**?

Where are its **spores** found?

Soft tree fern

This hardy tree fern has been popular for planting in the warm, wet regions of both Europe and North America since its introduction and cultivation in Europe in 1880. This species is not a tree at all but a true fern. However, its phenomenal popularity lies in the fact that it can reach treelike proportions.

Height 22 ft (7 m)

Width Up to 12 ft (4 m)

Leaf type Compound

Tree shape Columnar

Location Australia, Tasmania

New fronds unfurl from the top of the trunk in spring. The undersides of fronds have light brown, rounded spores dispersed at regular intervals.

The bark is chestnut brown, soft, and fibrous. It has a black, woody core.

Fossils show that soft tree ferns were around at the same time as the dinosaurs.

What **tree** is this?

Do the nuts have **smooth** or **spiny** husks?

Does it have **fragrant** flowers?

What part of the tree gives it its **name**?

The male and female catkins grow on **separate** trees. True or false?

Where in the **world** does it grow?

Golden chestnut

This broadly conical, evergreen tree is often referred to as the golden chinkapin and, sometimes botanically, as *Castanopsis chrysophylla*. This is incorrect as the male and female flowers on *Castanopsis* grow on separate catkins, whereas the male and female flowers on this tree are on the same catkin.

Height Up to 100 ft (30 m)

Width Up to 40 ft (12 m)

Leaf type Simple

Tree shape Conical

Location United States

Fragrant male and female flowers are borne on catkins in summer. These are followed by dense clusters of spiny husks, which contain glossy brown nuts.

The name golden chestnut comes from the golden hairs on the underside of its leaves.

Cup-shaped flowers

What **tree** is this?

How **wide** does it grow?

Is it **related** to the magnolia?

It was first cultivated in **France**. True or false?

What **shape** does it form?

Are the flower buds **hairy** or **smooth**?

Evergreens
Michelia doltsopa

Sweet michelia

This spreading tree is related to magnolia and was brought to the West by Scottish plant collector George Forrest when he came across it in Yunnan, China, in 1918. He sent seeds of the sweet michelia to Caerhays Castle in Cornwall, England, where they were first cultivated.

Height Up to 70 ft (20 m)

Width Up to 50 ft (15 m)

Leaf type Simple

Tree shape Spreading

Location China, Himalayas

The flower buds form in the fall and are covered in fine cinnamon-colored hairs. The buds open in spring to reveal cup-shaped flowers. Each flower is strongly scented, almost pungent, in an enclosed space or on hot spring days.

Sweet michelia branches appear brown because they are densely covered in brown hairs.

What **tree** is this?

Are its flowers a valuable source of **nectar** for insects?

How **high** does it grow?

It flowers in **January**. True or false?

Does it have **shiny** or **dull** leaves?

Does it always have **rough** bark?

It is the state flower of three **American** states. True or false?

Bull bay

Bull bay, also known as Southern magnolia, is indigenous to coastal United States. In warm, temperate areas, it develops into a tree with a broad canopy and short stems, and is a common sight in urban areas. In cooler regions, it is often grown as a wall shrub, where the combination of glossy, dark green foliage and creamy white flowers is dramatic.

Height 60–80 ft (18–25 m)

Width Up to 30 ft (10 m)

Leaf type Simple

Tree shape Varies

Location United States

The gray-brown bark is smooth at first, cracking into irregular small plates as it ages.

The bull bay is the state flower of Mississippi and Louisiana in the United States.

Flowers through summer and early fall provide a late source of nectar for insects, and are followed by seed pods with red seeds.

226

Graceful branches

What **tree** is this?

The fruit changes **color** three times as it ripens. True or false?

What **shape** does it form?

Does it have **weeping** or **upright** branches?

Does this tree have **aerial roots**?

Are the fruits **grouped** in sets of two or five?

This tree can be grown as a **houseplant**. True or false?

Evergreens
Ficus benjamina

Weeping fig

The graceful weeping fig has strongly ascending branches that weep (hang down) at the tips. In the tropics it is a broadly spreading, large evergreen tree. It is native to south and southeast Asia, north Australia, and the southwest Pacific, but has been widely cultivated throughout the tropics.

Height Up to 100 ft (30 m)

Width Up to 70 ft (20 m)

Leaf type Simple

Tree shape Weeping

Location Asia, Australia

The fruit is small rounded figs, which grow in pairs nearest the ends of the twigs. They ripen from green to pink, then turn scarlet before ripening to purple, and eventually black.

When the weeping fig is grown as a houseplant, it often drops all of its leaves if moved.

Like most fig trees, this tree is a stranger, developing aerial roots that descend to interlace the main trunk. The bark is pale gray, sometimes almost white.

Snake-like roots

What **tree** is this?

Where in the **world** does it grow?

Do its seeds **germinate** on the ground?

This tree **strangles** other trees. True or false?

What **insect** pollinates its flowers?

How do the **roots** help the tree to survive?

How **high** does it grow?

Evergreens
Ficus macrophylla

Moreton bay fig

This tree is indigenous to eastern Australia and New South Wales, as well as Lord Howe Island in the south. It is known as a strangler because its seedling germinates in the canopy of a host tree and lives on it, until its aerial roots touch the ground. Then it strangles its host and eventually takes its place as a freestanding tree itself.

Height Up to 200 ft (60 m)

Width Up to 200 ft (60 m)

Leaf type Simple

Tree shape Spreading

Location Australia

The tree develops magnificent snakelike roots. As well as helping it gather nutrients, the roots prevent the tree from toppling over.

The fruit is up to 1 in (2.5 cm) wide. It is green ripening to purple with lighter spots.

Fig flowers grow inside the fruit, where they are pollinated by fig wasps.

Stiltlike roots

What **tree** is this?

It can **desalinate** seawater. True or false?

Does it grow in **coastal** regions?

What **color** is its bark?

Does it provide **shelter** for fish?

Are its leaves **pointed** or **rounded**?

How **wide** does it grow?

Evergreens
Rhizophora mucronata

Asiatic mangrove

This broadly spreading, multistemmed evergreen tree is native to coastal regions of east Africa, India, southeast Asia, the western Pacific Islands, and northern Australia. It grows with its roots in salt water, which would kill most trees, but this tree has its own built-in desalination mechanism—the process of removing salt from seawater.

Height 30–80 ft (10–25 m)

Width Up to 50 ft (15 m)

Leaf type Simple

Tree shape Spreading

Location Asia, Africa, Oceania

The leaves have a sharply pointed tip and turn from green to red-brown.

The tree's stiltlike roots anchor it to the seabed. Many types of small fish also use the tangled roots for protection from predators.

The biggest mangrove forest in the world is the Sundarbans in the Bay of Bengal, southern Asia.

Leathery leaves

What **tree** is this?

Is it **hardy** or **tender**?

Does the flower have **seven** or **eleven** petals?

You can **carve** your name into the leaves. True or false?

Does it have **long-lasting** flowers?

What color are its **seeds**?

This tree produces **poisonous** fruit. True or false?

Evergreens
Clusia rosea

Autograph tree

This tree thrives in coastal regions, being tolerant of salt spray, high winds, and salty soil. Its common name refers to its leaves, which are so thick that words can be carved into them. The bark is light gray and smooth. The leathery leaves have a bright green upper surface that contrasts with their pale green underside.

Height Up to 50 ft (15 m)

Width Up to 50 ft (15 m)

Leaf type Simple

Tree shape Spreading

Location North America

The fruit are glossy green, globular capsules. When mature, they split to release small, orange-white seeds.

The autograph tree has poisonous fruit and toxic sap that can irritate skin.

Flowers consist of seven fleshy white petals surrounding a cluster of green-yellow stamens. They have a short life, opening in the late afternoon and beginning to turn brown and die by the following morning.

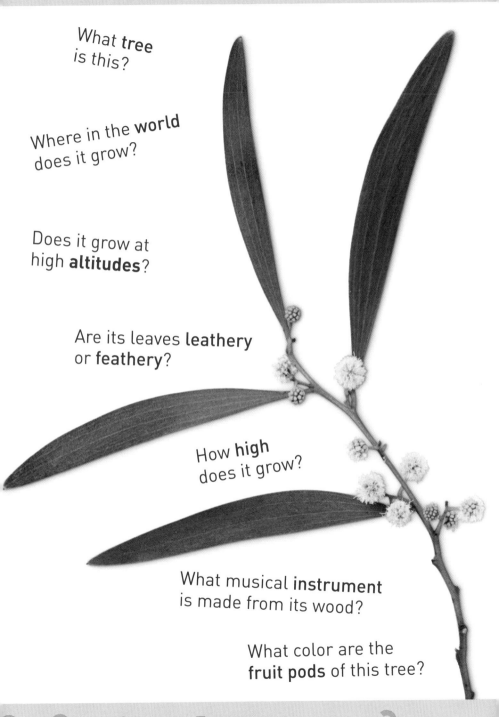

What **tree** is this?

Where in the **world** does it grow?

Does it grow at high **altitudes**?

Are its leaves **leathery** or **feathery**?

How **high** does it grow?

What musical **instrument** is made from its wood?

What color are the **fruit pods** of this tree?

Evergreens
Acacia melanoxylon

Blackwood acacia

Also known as the Australian blackwood, this pyramid-shaped tree reaches up to 130 ft (40 m) in height, although it normally remains much shorter. It has a range that extends from southern Queensland to central Tasmania. It grows at 3,280 ft (1,000 m) above sea level in the Tasmanian rainforest.

Height Up to 130 ft (40 m)

Width Up to 70 ft (20 m)

Leaf type Varies

Tree shape Conical

Location Australia, Tasmania

Bipinnate young leaves give the tree a feathery appearance.

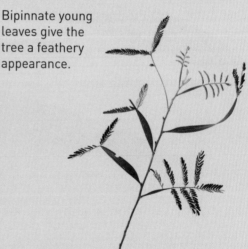

Blackwood acacia wood has good acoustic qualities and is used to make violins.

The mildly fragrant flowers grow on panicles (branched flower stalks) and are followed by reddish-brown fruit pods that contain flat, rounded seeds.

What **tree** is this?

Where in the **world** does it grow?

What **shape** does it form?

How many **petals** do its flowers have?

Is it **deciduous** outside its native range?

What time of year does it **flower**?

Are the leaves of this tree **shiny** or **dull**?

Evergreens
Eucryphia glutinosa

Eucryphia

This small, neat tree is evergreen in its native Chile but usually deciduous in cultivation in Europe. It has a broadly columnar form, with a mass of strongly vertical branches. Eucryphia, sometimes known as the brush bush, was introduced into western cultivation in 1859, and is a beautiful flowering tree.

Height 20–30 ft (6–10 m)

Width Up to 20 ft (6 m)

Leaf type Compound

Tree shape Columnar

Location Chile

The four-petaled flowers, which are about 2½ in (6 cm) wide, emerge in late summer.

Each leaflet has a prominent wavy margin, a shiny dark green upper surface, and a pale green underside.

Masses of white flowers cover the upright trees, making them look like white pillars.

238

Pear-shaped fruit

What **tree** is this?

Is it a **fast-growing** tree?

Where was it first **cultivated**?

What **color** skin does the fruit have?

Is the **fruit** rich in minerals and oils?

The fruit was **called** alligator pears. True or false?

Avocado

More than 10,000 years ago, people in Mexico and Central America gathered and ate the fruit of wild avocado trees, and it didn't take long before they started to cultivate this nutritious fruit, which is rich in minerals and oils. Today, the fast-growing avocado is still cultivated in Mexico and Central America, where the trees thrive in consistently high temperatures.

Height Up to 70 ft (20 m)

Width Up to 30 ft (10 m)

Leaf type Alternate simple

Tree shape Broadly spreading

Location Mexico, Central America

The tree, which typically has a short trunk before it begins to branch, has smooth, dark gray bark that becomes fissured with age.

The pear-shaped fruit has leathery green to purple-brown outer skin. In the 16th century, the Tlaxcalans in Central Mexico greeted the arrival of Spanish explorers with baskets of avocados and offerings of other local food.

Old names for avocados include alligator pears and shell pears.

What **tree** is this?

Where in the **world** does it grow?

Is it a **large** or **small** tree?

How **high** does it grow?

How much does the fruit **weigh**?

Each fruit contains as many as 20 **seeds**. True or false?

The fruit is easy to **open**. True or false?

Semi-evergreens
Bertholletia excelsa

Brazil nut tree

This large, semi-evergreen tree is native to Brazil, but it also inhabits other countries bordering the Amazon basin. It is a typical emergent rainforest tree—standing above the canopy with a long, straight, branchless trunk for two-thirds of its length. It is topped by a crown made up of long branches with dark foliage.

Height Up to 130 ft (40 m)

Width Up to 100 ft (30 m)

Leaf type Simple

Tree shape Spreading

Location South America

The fruit of the Brazil nut tree is the size of a grapefruit and weighs up to 4½ lbs (2 kg). It has a hard, woody exterior like a coconut. Neatly packed inside each fruit are about 25 hard-shelled seeds known as Brazil nuts.

The bark is light gray, smooth when young, and cracks vertically in maturity.

Large rodents called agoutis are the only mammals with strong enough teeth to crack open Brazil nut fruits.

Sacred tree

What **tree** is this?

What other **name** is it called?

How **high** does it grow?

What color is its **ripe** fruit?

Which **religions** believe this is a sacred tree?

Is it a **long**- or **short**-lived species?

Bo tree

This long-lived species (some specimens are believed to be 2,000 years old) is sacred to both Buddhists and Hindus, and is usually grown close to temples. Its native habitat extends from India and Pakistan to Indonesia, but it is widely planted in other regions, including subtropical areas of the United States.

Height 50–100 ft (15–30 m)

Width Up to 100 ft (30 m)

Leaf type Simple

Tree shape Spreading

Location Asia

The fruit is a small, green fig, ripening to purple. It grows in rounded and stalkless clusters along the twigs.

An ancient bo tree in Sri Lanka is said to have grown from a cutting from Buddha's tree of enlightenment.

According to Buddhist beliefs, the Buddha attained spiritual enlightenment under the bo tree, also known as the sacred fig.

What **tree** is this?

Where in the **world** does it grow?

What **colour** do its leaves turn in the dry season?

Which **product** is made from this tree?

How did the ancient Mayas and Aztecs use the **sap**?

Rubber tree

This fast-growing, broadly columnar tree is indigenous to both the Amazon River basin in Brazil and the Orinoco River basin in Venezuela. It has been widely planted elsewhere in tropical regions, such as in Malaysia, because it is the main source of natural rubber for commercial use.

Height Up to 130 ft (40 m)

Width Up to 70 ft (20 m)

Leaf type Compound

Tree shape Columnar

Location South America

Rubber can be tapped from the trees when they are six years old. This is done by cutting a slanting groove in the outer bark and allowing the milky white latex to ooze out into a collecting cup.

The ancient Maya and Aztecs used the sap to make rubber balls and shoes.

The leaves are dark green on the upper surface. They may turn orange-red and fall in the dry season.

Prickly giant

What **tree** is this?

This tree is also known as the **silk-cotton tree**. True or false?

Does it have **fragrant** or **foul-smelling** flowers?

How **high** does it grow?

The **thorns** on the bark never drop off. True or false?

What **lifesaving** device is made from fibers surrounding the seeds?

Does it have to be cut down to **harvest** the seeds?

Kapok

Many rainforest trees grow to great heights and display huge buttress roots. Few, though, are more impressive than the majestic kapok. This important canopy species can grow as high as 230 ft (70 m), with buttresses that project up to 65 ft (20 m) from the trunk. Its flowers open at night and emit a foul odor that attracts bats, its main pollinators.

Height Up to 230 ft (70 m)

Width Up to 70 ft (20 m)

Leaf type Compound

Tree shape Spreading

Location Asia, Africa, the Americas

The short, thick thorns on kapok trunks are a formidable natural defense mechanism against animals that would otherwise eat the tree's bark. The thorns eventually drop off as the tree ages.

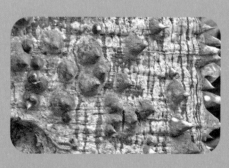

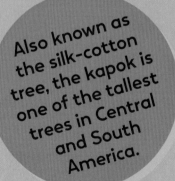

Also known as the silk-cotton tree, the kapok is one of the tallest trees in Central and South America.

A kapok tree produces seed pods covered in white fluff that are harvested without cutting down the tree. The fibers are used as stuffing for pillows, mattresses, and even life jackets.

What **tree** is this?

Where in the **world** does it grow?

Is this tree **endangered** in the wild?

Are the leaves **leathery** or **frondlike**?

The dried seed pods make a **rattling** sound when they are shaken. True or false?

Does this tree have very **long** seed pods?

Semi-evergreens
Delonix regia

Flamboyant tree

This tree originates from Madagascar, where it is now endangered in the wild. However, the flamboyant tree is widely cultivated across tropical and subtropical regions of the world as an ornamental tree. It is also known as the flame tree, and in India, *gulmohar*, which translates from Hindi as "peacock flowers," a reference to its showy, orange-red flowers.

Height Up to 70 ft (20 m)

Width Up to 70 ft (20 m)

Leaf type Compound

Tree shape Spreading

Location Madagascar

The leaves are frondlike, similar to those of the jacaranda. They have a bright green upper surface and a paler underside.

The dried seed pods are sometimes called "shak-shak"; when shaken they make a rattling sound similar to maracas.

The flowers are followed by flattened seed pods, which grow up to 24 in (60 cm) long and hang from branches; green at first, ripening to brown.

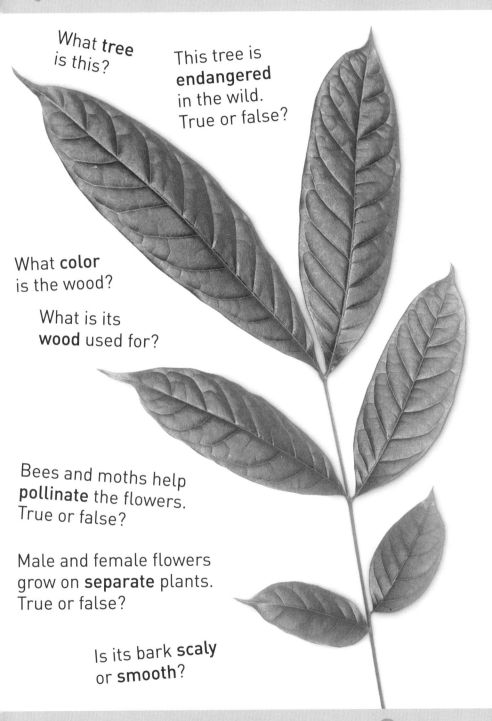

What **tree** is this?

This tree is **endangered** in the wild. True or false?

What **color** is the wood?

What is its **wood** used for?

Bees and moths help **pollinate** the flowers. True or false?

Male and female flowers grow on **separate** plants. True or false?

Is its bark **scaly** or **smooth**?

Semi-evergreens
Swietenia mahagoni

Mahogany

Mahogany is a semi-evergreen tree with upward-sweeping branches. It has dense wood, which has a rich, red color. The tree has male and female flowers on the same plant. After fertilization by bees and moths, the fruits develop slowly. Unfortunately, due to overcutting, mahogany is now endangered in the wild.

Height Up to 70 ft (20 m)

Width Up to 70 ft (20 m)

Leaf type Compound

Tree shape Columnar

Location Central America, Caribbean

The mahogany's trunk may become buttressed with age. Its bark is dark red-brown and scaly.

This tree is probably best known as the source of one of the world's most valued woods, which is used to make furniture.

Mahogany wood is often used in musical instruments.

Glossary

Aril
Coat that covers some seeds;
often fleshy and bright.

Bract
Modified leaf at the base of a flower or
flowerhead. A bract may be small and
scalelike, or large and petallike, or it
may resemble normal foliage.

Burr
1. Prickly, spiny, or hooked fruit,
seedhead, or flowerhead.
2. Woody outgrowth on the trunk
of some trees.

Buttress
Trunk base that is fluted or swollen,
giving stability to a tree in shallow
soil conditions.

Catkin
A type of flower cluster, usually
hanging, in which scalelike bracts and
tiny flowers are arranged in a spike.

Conifer
A large woody, sometimes massive
seed tree that has its reproductive
parts arranged in shoots called strobili,
or cones, instead of flowers. Most are
evergreen and have small but very
tough, needlelike leaves.

Cultivar
Another word for "cultivated variety."
A cultivated plant that keeps distinct
characteristics when propagated (bred).

Deciduous
A tree that loses its leaves and remains
leafless for some months of the year,
usually in winter (temperate zones) or
the dry season (tropical zones).

Evergreen
A tree that bears leaves throughout
the year.

Form
Any variant of a species.

Frond
A large compound leaf, especially
of a fern or palm.

Hybrid
Offspring produced from parents of
different species. Hybrids show new
characteristics. Hybrid names include
the names of both parent species
separated by an "x," such as
Aesculus x carnea.

Indigenous
Also called native, a species that
occurs naturally in a particular region.

Panicle
An elongated, branched flower cluster
with stalked flowers.

Pinna (plural Pinnae)
One of the main divisions of a
featherlike compound leaf, such as
a fern frond.

Pollen
Tiny grains produced by seed plants that contain male gametes (sex cells) for fertilizing the female egg.

Semi-evergreen
A tree that loses its leaves for only a short period during the year or that sheds a proportion of its leaves periodically but is never entirely leafless.

Species
In biological classification, a species is a group of similar plants (or other living things such as animals) that can usually interbreed. The species name is on the front page for each tree in this book.

Spore
A single cell containing half the quantity of genetic material of typical body cells. Unlike gametes (sex cells), spores can divide and grow without being fertilized. Tree ferns are the only trees that reproduce by spores.

Whorl
An arrangement of several identical structural parts in a circle around the same point.

Index

Acknowledgments

For Smithsonian Enterprises
Avery Naughton, Licensing Coordinator; Paige Towler,
Editorial Lead; Jill Corcoran, Senior Director, Licensed Publishing;
Brigid Ferraro, Vice President of New Business and Licensing;
Carol LeBlanc, President

The publisher would like to thank the following for their kind
permission to reproduce their photographs:
(Key: a-above; b-below/bottom; c-center; f-far; l-left; r-right; t-top)

5 Dorling Kinderseley: Thomas Marent. 6 Dorling Kindersley: Chris
Hornbecker / Ryan Neil (crb). 14 Dorling Kindersley: Gary Ombler / Royal
Botanic Gardens, Kew (tl). 15 Dorling Kindersley: Gary Ombler / Batsford
Garden Centre and Arboretum. 16 Alamy Stock Photo: Paul R. Sterry /
Nature Photographers Ltd (cl). Dorling Kindersley: Gary Ombler /
Batsford Garden Centre and Arboretum (br). 18 Dreamstime.com: Heiti
Paves (br); Ricochet69 (cl). 20 Getty Images / iStock: Richard-P-Long
(bl). 22 Shutterstock.com: Martin Fowler (br). 23 Dreamstime.com:
Yarablimm25. 24 Alamy Stock Photo: Inga Spence (br). 26 Getty Images
/ iStock: ErikAgar (br); pcturner71 (bl). 27 Dreamstime.com:
Marinadenisenko. 28 Dreamstime.com: Ken Griffiths (cl). Getty Images /
iStock: Jon Benedictus (br). 29 Dorling Kindersley: Gary Ombler /
Batsford Garden Centre and Arboretum. 30 Dorling Kindersley: Gary
Ombler / Batsford Garden Centre and Arboretum (cl). 36 Dorling
Kindersley: Neil Fletcher (bl). 37 Shutterstock.com: David Clinnick. 38
Dreamstime.com: Steven Prorak (bl); Dzmitry Zelianeuski (br). 42
Dorling Kindersley: A. D. Schilling (cl). 44 Alamy Stock Photo: Yvette
Cardozo (br). Dreamstime.com: Marinadenisenko (cl). 50 Dreamstime.
com: David Pillow (br). 53 Shutterstock.com: KanphotoSS. 56
Dreamstime.com: Zoran Sretovi (bc). 58 Getty Images / iStock: stockcam
/ E+ (br). 60 Dreamstime.com: Viktoria Ivanets (br). 62 Getty Images /
iStock: NataBaiborodina (bl). 64 Alamy Stock Photo: blickwinkel /
fotototo (br). Dreamstime.com: David Máška (bl). 66 Depositphotos Inc:
nbiebach (bl). 67 Dorling Kindersley: Gary Ombler / Royal Botanic
Gardens, Kew. 68 Dorling Kindersley: Gary Ombler / Westonbirt, The
National Arboretum (br). 71 Dreamstime.com: Elise Pearlstine. 72
Dreamstime.com: Ecophoto (cl); Shariqkhan (br). 74 Shutterstock.com:
Maria Kovalets (cl). 76 Getty Images / iStock: Alexander Denisenko (cr);
saraTM (cl). 78 Dreamstime.com: Puttsk (br). 82 Dorling Kindersley:
Peter Anderson (br). Dreamstime.com: Olena Stefiuk (cl). 83 Dorling
Kindersley: Gary Ombler / Batsford Garden Centre and Arboretum. 84
Dorling Kindersley: Gary Ombler / Batsford Garden Centre and
Arboretum (cl). 86 Dorling Kindersley: Gary Ombler / Westonbirt, The
National Arboretum (crb). 88 Dreamstime.com: Petrsalinger (cl); Teresa
Virbickis (crb). 90 Dreamstime.com: Eugenesergeev (cr); Damian Pawlos
(br). 92 Getty Images / iStock: Ornitolog82 (br). 94 Dreamstime.com:
Mikelane45 (crb). 96 Dreamstime.com: Dachux21 (br); Hellmann1 (cl).
98 Dorling Kindersley: Peter Anderson (br). Getty Images / iStock: Brilt
(bl). 99 Dorling Kindersley: Gary Ombler / Westonbirt, The National
Arboretum. 104 Dorling Kindersley: Gary Ombler / Batsford Garden
Centre and Arboretum (cl). 105 Alamy Stock Photo: Frank Blackburn.
106 Dreamstime.com: Michael Smith (br). Getty Images / iStock:
ksushsh (cl). 108 Dreamstime.com: Yorozu Kitamura (bl); Nahhan (br).
110 123RF.com: neydt (br). Shutterstock.com: Peter Turner
Photography (cl). 112 Shutterstock.com: Riska Parakeet (crb). 116
Shutterstock.com: Yuttana Joe (cl). 118 Alamy Stock Photo: Circa
Images / Glasshouse Images (bl). 120 Dreamstime.com: Hiroshi
Ichikawa (cl). 121 Shutterstock.com: Mathisa. 122 Dreamstime.com:
Filipfoto25 (br); Ncristian (cl). 124 Dreamstime.com: Bubushonok (cl).
126 Dorling Kindersley: Neil Fletcher (bl). 127 Dorling Kindersley: Mark
Winwood / RHS Wisley. 128 Alamy Stock Photo: Heritage Image

Partnership Ltd (c). 130 Dorling Kindersley: Mark Winwood / RHS Wisley
(br). 131 Dreamstime.com: Juan Moyano. 132 Dreamstime.com:
Natalyka (cl). 134 Alamy Stock Photo: Adam Eastland Art + Architecture
(cl). 136 Dreamstime.com: Anest (br); Axel Bueckert (cl). 138
Dreamstime.com: Pepperboxdesign (cl); Zoli153 (br). 142 Dreamstime.
com: Nikolai Kurzenko (br). 144 Dreamstime.com: Tamara Kulikova
(crb); Nahhan (cl). 146 Dreamstime.com: Whiskybottle (clb). 148
Depositphotos Inc: phil_bird (br). Dreamstime.com: Dmitry Potashkin
(cl). 150 Dreamstime.com: Wirestock (cl). 151 Dreamstime.com:
Debu55y. 152 Dreamstime.com: Steven Cukrov (cl); Irinafuks (cr);
Simona Pavan (br). 154 Dreamstime.com: Natalia Bachkova (cl). 156
123RF.com: Erich Teister (cl). Dreamstime.com: Nahhan (br). 158
Dreamstime.com: Simona Pavan (crb). 160 Dreamstime.com: Anest (br).
162 123RF.com: zosimus (br). Dreamstime.com: Philip Bird (cl). 164
123RF.com: damann (br). Dreamstime.com: Dadalia (cl). 166
Shutterstock.com: Jim and Lynne Weber (br). 167 Dreamstime.com:
Tamara Kulikova. 168 Dreamstime.com: Agustin Vai (cl). 170
Shutterstock.com: guentermanaus (br). 172 Getty Images / iStock:
mtreasure (cl). 174 Shutterstock.com: ANCH (cl). 178 Shutterstock.com:
Viniciussouza06 (cl). 179 Dorling Kindersley: Gary Ombler / Royal
Botanic Gardens, Kew. 180 Dreamstime.com: Dimarik16 (cl). 181
Dorling Kindersley: Gary Ombler / Royal Botanic Gardens, Kew. 182
Shutterstock.com: Plalo S (br). 183 Dorling Kindersley: Gary Ombler /
Royal Botanic Gardens, Kew. 184 Dreamstime.com: Rudra Narayan
Mitra (crb); Devindar Shinde (bl). 185 Dorling Kindersley: Gary Ombler /
Batsford Garden Centre and Arboretum. 186 Dreamstime.com:
Armando Frazão (clb). 189 Dorling Kindersley: Colin Keates / Natural
History Museum, London. 190 Alamy Stock Photo: Wildlife Gmbh (br).
194 Alamy Stock Photo: FLPA (cl). Dreamstime.com: Steve Ball (bl).
196 Shutterstock.com: Peter Turner Photography (br). 198 Dreamstime.
com: Immphoto94 (cl); Sunnirae (br). 202 Shutterstock.com: Bob Pool
(cl). 204 Dorling Kindersley: Gary Ombler / Westonbirt, The National
Arboretum (cl). 206 Dreamstime.com: Nkarol (cl). 208 Dreamstime.com:
Albertoloyo (b). 210 Dreamstime.com: Olya Solodenko (br). 211
Dreamstime.com: Daniel Poloha. 212 Dorling Kindersley: Gary Ombler /
Royal Botanic Gardens, Kew. Dreamstime.com: Olya Solodenko (cl).
213 Dreamstime.com: Somchai Meewichai. 214 123RF.com: Karandaev
(cr). Dreamstime.com: Tasakorn Kongmoon (cl); Mansum008 (br). 215
Dorling Kindersley: Gary Ombler / Royal Botanic Gardens, Kew. 216
Dreamstime.com: Mai Moolsom (b). 217 Dreamstime.com: Kickboy24.
218 Dreamstime.com: Donyanedomam (br); Supamas Lhakjit (cl). 222
Shutterstock.com: StephenVanHove (b). 223 Shutterstock.com:
Gardens by Design. 224 Dreamstime.com: Pstedrak (b). 226
Dreamstime.com: Helga11 (br); Dmitry Potashkin (cl). 227 Getty Images
/ iStock: grafvision. 228 Dreamstime.com: Supawit Srethbhakdi (br).
Shutterstock.com: TBamphoto (cl). 230 Shutterstock.com: Rosamar
(br). 231 Alamy Stock Photo: blickwinkel / K. Wothe. 232 123RF.com:
sarapon (cl). Dreamstime.com: Seadam (br). 233 Getty Images / iStock:
passion4nature. 234 Dreamstime.com: Francisco Alberto Rodriguez
Hernandez (br); Patcharamai Vutipapornkul (cl). 236 Shutterstock.com:
Victoria Tucholka (cl). 238 Shutterstock.com: Tom Curtis (cl). 240
Dorling Kindersley: The Royal Botanic Gardens, Kew (cr). 241 Alamy
Stock Photo: Foto Arena LTDA. 244 Getty Images / iStock: nuwatphoto
(br). Shutterstock.com: Kaninw (cl). 246 Shutterstock.com: Kidsada
Manchinda (cl); Likit Supasai (br). 249 Dreamstime.com: Decha
Somparn. 250 Dreamstime.com: Carlos Miguel (cr); Paco Toscano
Santana (br). 251 Shutterstock.com: Sutana4. 252 Dreamstime.com:
Photographyfirm (br); Jaka Suryanta (cl).

All other images © Dorling Kindersley Limited